hristmas 2010 from Judy

$5.—

USED AIRCRAFT GUIDE

USED AIRCRAFT GUIDE

Jeff Ethell

Charles Scribner's Sons
New York

Library of Congress Cataloging in Publication Data
Ethell, Jeffrey L.
  Used aircraft guide.
  Includes index.
    1. Used aircraft. 2. Airplanes—Purchasing.
I. Title.
TL724.E83   629.133′34   78-31383
ISBN 0-684-16067-6

1 3 5 7 9 11 13 15 17 19   M/C   20 18 16 14 12 10 8 6 4 2

Printed in the United States of America

Opening page: The Bellanca Viking 300.
Title page: The Twin Comanche.
Above: The Cessna 170.

Acknowledgments

Without question much credit will go to the author that deserves to be placed elsewhere, for without a great deal of help in this often confusing maze of used aircraft, this book would not have been written.

First, to Joe Christy, fellow aviation writer and, in many ways, mentor to the author. Without question Joe is one of the foremost experts on general aviation aircraft and his files and talents were placed at my disposal.

Chuck Proctor, First Atlas Aircraft Sales at Chesterfield County Airport, Virginia, spent hours with the author deciphering used aircraft prices and their meaning on his own time, helping to define the word *average* in pricing airplanes.

Jim Gunter of the Virginia Division of Aeronautics and Don Eiler of Don Eiler's Custom Photography in Richmond came through with photos of aircraft that the author could not track down. Both of these enthusiastic pilots not only produced the photos, but did so in record time when the author's deadline was far behind.

Several aircraft manufacturers sent photos and data on their used products, and I would be remiss in not thanking them for doing so when the real goal of any company is to sell new products, not used ones: Frank Pedroja of Beech Aircraft Corporation, Dean Humphrey of Cessna Aircraft Company, B. A. Waltrip of Grumman American Aviation Corporation (before it became Gulfstream American), Mike Murrell of Piper Aircraft Corporation, and James F. Wright of Ted Smith Aerostar Corporation (before it was sold to Piper).

To all of them, my warmest thanks. May the result be worth their efforts.

Jeff Ethell

Contents

Preface

The boom in private and business flying, which began almost imperceptibly in the late sixties, was clearly discernible by 1973, and has accelerated since, has been variously attributed to the businessman's growing awareness of the company-owned plane's competitive advantages, the 55-mile-per-hour highway speed limit, and the airlines' reduced number of flights to a shrinking number of domestic airports.

But those of us who have grown up with civil aviation since World War II see at least two additional factors, without which those listed above would not matter very much. First, modern light aircraft have evolved into extremely reliable, comfortable machines that may be safely operated by any reasonably normal person possessing a modicum of common sense; and second, advances in electronics have given today's private pilot magical navigational systems that eliminate both the work and the guesswork in cross-country flying.

Perhaps the great increase in new-plane sales is owed in part to each of the above factors, plus some the experts have not considered. It is certain that most new civilian aircraft purchased are used for business (and, of course, are subject to the same tax write-offs as all other business machines).

For every new airplane sold in the civil market, at least six used ones find new owners. And since a high percentage of those buying their first airplane start with a used machine, a survey of the used aircraft market, along with a discussion of its pitfalls, and tips learned from years of exposure to this market, should prove useful.

In short, if you are contemplating the purchase of a used lightplane, this book will save you time, money, and doubt.

1

Accentuate the Negative

The only realistic approach to the purchase of a used plane is one of extreme caution. True, you may well be dealing with a totally honorable person; but that does not really matter, because he may be offering you a problem, or an incipient problem, without knowing it. Most people with used airplanes for sale will act in good faith, but that is no guarantee that they do not innocently possess a stolen machine or one with an unsuspected mechanical defect. If the seller bought in the used market, he could unknowingly have a rebuild or even a craft with a lien against it that has not yet surfaced. Usually, however, the unanticipated or hidden problems will be mechanical in nature.

I will list procedures for uncovering these and other potential booby traps, but first a few preliminary considerations.

Buy Practically

Too many pilots, when buying an airplane, tend to select the machine they most admire rather than one that will give them the most utility. Clearly, if you are to enjoy maximum use of your plane, it must be suited to the kind of flying you do, and it should not require a degree of skill to operate that is beyond your level of experience.

So, be honest with yourself. Take an objective view of your flying experience to date, and choose an airplane that does not "tense you up" to fly it. Acquire the experience first, then trade up to a plane with more

Chances are, the seller is acting in good faith; but his airplane may have an incipient mechanical problem he does not know about.

muscle. Reverse this procedure, and you will find yourself flying less and enjoying it less, while your beautiful flying machine—which seems to challenge, rather than invite, you to fly—sits in the hangar consuming the fixed costs of ownership that accrue whether a plane is flown or not.

Of equal importance is the need to match your airplane with the kind of flying you do. For example, if you expect to utilize your aircraft for frequent cross-country trips, that should rule out a low-horsepower two-place craft. The small two-placers trade speed, range, and load-carrying ability for economy. All things are relative, of course, but an extended flight in an airplane that cruises at less than 2 miles per minute is sort of like driving a turnpike at 40 miles per hour.

On the other hand, the minimum-cost two-placer can be highly practical for the weekend pilot who merely seeks a few hours of hassle-free fun flying on nice days.

Another consideration is the type and amount of radio equipment offered with a used plane. Some of these black boxes are capable of wondrous feats in the science of navigation, continuous speed and distance readouts, etc. But aircraft electronics *(avionics)* are expensive both in first cost and in maintenance, so there is no point in paying for DME (distance-measuring equipment), marker beacon, and a glide scope receiver unless your kind of flying can make good use of it all.

Resale

Of prime importance is a reasonably accurate estimate of what a given used plane is going to be worth two or three years hence, because its value when you sell or trade will determine what it has cost you to own it. In recent years, the twin forces of inflation and growing demand have almost kept up with the normal depreciation of light aircraft; and in fact there is a cutoff point at which well-maintained airplanes suffer little or no further depreciation—and in some cases actually increase in value until they bring as much as they did when new.

There are plenty of pitfalls, however. If your plane is fabric-covered, estimating its worth, say, 1,200 flying hours from now may be very difficult. In most cases it is very hard to judge how long fabric will last. If fabric condition is very good, that may be determined with some accuracy, and with proper care, you may reasonably expect it to remain that way for two or three more years if the fabric is cotton, perhaps a little longer if linen. But most used planes with cotton fabric will not test in "high green" with a punch tester, or near 80 pounds tensile strength (minimum specs when new). Most will range downward from there, leaving one in an area of great uncertainty.

Cost will not be your only concern if your "rag-wing" needs re-covering. Finding a shop that will do it right is not easy, because the trade schools are not turning out aircraft mechanics nowadays who have any real experience in aircraft dope and fabric work. They are fond of saying that it is a dying art, because only a few fabric-covered airplanes—sport planes—are still in production.

9

The average re-covering job will cost somewhere around $3,500. You can save up to 80 percent of this by doing the job yourself; but Federal Aviation Regulations (FARs) require that such work be done under the supervision of a licensed aircraft mechanic. And you will need a proper place to work, well ventilated, with an electrical source and temperature control. The major items of expense (excluding labor) will be for about 50 yards of fabric at $5 to $7 per yard currently, and up to 35 gallons of dope at about $8 per gallon for prime and filler coats and about $16 per gallon for color.

Until fairly recently, cotton was the principal fabric used for aircraft covering, and it is still favored by many veteran aircraftsmen because it finishes out so beautifully and is easy to repair. When properly finished with butyrate dope, it should last for six to eight years if the airplane is hangared. Sun is fabric's worst enemy, and the upper wing surfaces are usually the first to go.

Similarly finished and cared for, linen should last a little longer, but both cotton and linen now cost 20–30 percent more than the longer-lasting synthetics, the so-called "lifetime" exterior coverings. The Dacrons such as Stits Poly-Fiber, Ceconite, and Eonnex will retain their strengths (about twice that of cotton) indefinitely when properly finished and maintained. They will, in fact, last longer than is necessary because the internal structure will need refurbishing after, say, fifteen years or so. The chrome-moly steel tubing in the fuselage will probably have acquired some rust, and possibly a small crack or two; aluminum-alloy members may have some corrosion; load-carrying fittings must be carefully inspected; and wood will usually need some sanding and revarnishing after such a span of time.

True, you may have no intention of keeping an airplane for fifteen years before trading—two or three years is a more realistic expectation—but what you are able to get for it when you sell or trade determines what it has cost to own. Three years from now, your new cotton fabric will probably test somewhat below 80 pounds tensile strength, while three-year-old Dacron will in most cases continue to test well above 100 pounds. This can easily make a $2,000 difference in what your plane will bring in the used market.

Airplanes are not affected by age and mileage as are cars. If you fly only 20 hours per month, that is 36,000 miles per year, assuming an average speed of 150 miles per hour. And an airplane with only 1,000 hours on it may be relatively new even though it has already covered 150,000 miles. Most automobiles have been consigned to the junk heap by then.

If you are considering a cotton-covered aircraft, you should know that sometimes the doped finish will deteriorate but the fabric beneath will still be fairly good. In such cases, a dope rejuvenator may be applied. But if the fabric is in poor condition, rejuvenation of the finish is of course a waste of money. And beware of fabric-covered airplanes with enamel finishes. Enamel is heavy; it hardens and cracks, is difficult to patch, and cannot be rejuvenated. Also, enamel is sometimes used on fabric that is in borderline condition (to skin by just one more annual inspection), because it looks good and is cheaper than dope rejuvenation.

10

Each of the synthetic fabrics has its own recommended finishing process. Stits Poly-Fiber sealed with resin and finished with two-part polyurethanes is probably the most durable. Ceconite Dacron is finished in conventional butyrate dope. Eonnex is precoated and has but three finish coats, two of emulsion and a gloss-sealer. Razorback glass cloth is also precoated but is usually finished with nontautening butyrate dope. All the synthetics weigh near (or slightly below) 4 ounces per square yard, which is the same as grade-A aircraft cotton. Eonnex offers a significant weight saving because of its three-coat finish, compared to the usual eight to twelve coats.

Wood is not used much anymore in the construction of airplanes, except in homebuilts and in Bellanca wings. Actually, Sitka spruce is an excellent airframe material, perhaps better than metal in some ways, especially when a wing is built as Bellanca does it to obtain unusual strength with light weight and then effectively sealed against moisture (it is resin-dipped). But wood does not lend itself well to modern production techniques. A wooden wing must be made by hand, whereas metal-framed wings are merely assembled from stamped and machined parts. Bellanca is able to stick with its less efficient approach because it builds only about 100 Vikings per year.

Age alone does little to aircraft-grade Sitka spruce. A lot of antique airplanes, dating back forty years or more, are safely flying with it. With proper care, the wood-winged airplane will last as long as any other, and there are enough early Mooneys, Beech Staggerwings, and Fairchild 24s around to prove it.

If you are considering the purchase of an older, wood-winged airplane, the most likely places to look for deterioration are under metal fittings, in tight or poorly ventilated spots where moisture could collect, and in oil-soaked areas. Moisture is sometimes trapped inside the wing along the trailing edge if there are an insufficient number of drain grommets (seaplane drain grommets are best if you fly in humid areas, because each creates a tiny suction that aids internal wing ventilation).

Most homebuilt airplanes have wooden wing structures, and a few have wood-framed fuselages. If you are tempted to buy a homebuilt, contact the Federal Aviation Agency (FAA) inspector who checked the work on it as it was being built. He will have had to okay the project from beginning to end, and his opinion will be valuable. In any case, each homebuilt must be individually judged, and in every case its value will be difficult to determine.

Marketability Factors

The factors which determine the value of a used plane are overall condition, engine time, major damage history, avionics installations, and estimated future rate of depreciation.

Total airframe time may be considered but is of much less importance if an airplane has received proper maintenance. A recent study reveals that the average maximum time that light aircraft are kept in service is 4,500 hours, with some remaining active up to 6,000 hours of flying time (assuming an average speed of only 125 miles per hour, that is 750,000 miles!). But

11

many—perhaps most—private pilots fly no more than 300 hours per year, and there are lots of lightplanes around that are fifteen years old with less than 2,000 hours on them. The airplane is such an efficient compressor of time and distance that the economics of ownership really cannot be compared with those of automobile ownership.

Confirm significant maintenance and repair items listed in the logs.

The phrase *good overall condition* covers a lot of things and is a judgment that must wait upon a careful inspection of the plane and its logs. A lot of buyers perform this inspection themselves, and the next chapter will list the procedures to be followed for a do-it-yourself inspection. I do, however, strongly recommend that you have this inspection done by an experienced aircraft mechanic, one with an inspector's rating (AI, or Aircraft Inspector), and of course one who has no interest in the deal. You will have to pay him $50 to $100 for his services, but he may save you many times that. He will, in almost every instance, notice things that you as a pilot are apt to overlook. He will immediately recognize a rebuilt airframe, and he will often spot developing problems that spell expense at some future date.

Still, there are advantages in doing the inspection yourself—if you are willing to invest the time and effort to do a thorough job. You will certainly know your airplane better if you do, and this in turn promotes good maintenance, which translates into safer, more worry-free flying.

Actually, your presale inspection of an aircraft is whatever you wish to make it. There is no law that compels you to do it right. But, clearly, you will either invest your time and effort, hire it done, or gamble.

Now, an airplane's Airworthiness Certificate, which by law must be displayed in the aircraft at all times, is maintained in force by means of the annual inspection, which must be performed by a licensed aircraft mechanic. In addition, planes flown for hire must have regular 100-hour inspections. The annual inspection, properly done, includes a certain amount of servicing.

Sometimes the seller may offer to include a fresh annual with the sale, but whether or not you will want to substitute this for your own independent inspection depends upon how much you want to know about your purchase. The annual inspection simply certifies that, as of the date performed, the airplane is airworthy (according to the FAA's definition of that term) and presumably will remain so, with proper maintenance, for another year. An annual properly done is a reasonable guarantee of a plane's overall condition—"properly done" because among aircraft mechanics, as in other trades, there are always a few dope-offs and incompetents. Generally speaking, however, APs (mechanics) and AIs (inspectors) possess a decent amount of personal integrity and are not inclined to risk their hard-won licenses with shoddy work. Most are also a mite independent. One once told me that his charge for performing an annual inspection would be "seventy-five dollars if I do it alone; one hundred dollars if you want to help."

"Engine time" is an important factor when considering a used plane. The average lightplane engine overhaul costs between $3,000 and $4,000 today, and since 1,900 hours is the average limit for a well-maintained engine before major overhaul is necessary, this is one of the first things you should check. But there is nothing really positive about it, and subtracting actual engine time from the manufacturer's "recommended time between overhaul" (TBO) is no guarantee of the amount of time left in an engine before this expense will have to be faced. If the airplane has been used for training, hauling sky divers, or doing other things that imposed a disproportionate amount of high-rpm time on it, then engine time cannot be safely stretched to its normal span. Therefore, it is certainly worthwhile to determine how an airplane has been used before you buy it.

According to FARs, the "damage history" of an airplane must be recorded in its logs. The airframe and engine logbooks are legal documents, and the FAA can be mightily offended by serious misrepresentations in them. It has the power to punish substantially those guilty of such deceptions. Still, you cannot accept all log entries as gospel. People are people, and some fudging creeps in. All maintenance, modifications, additions of equipment, and the like are recorded in the logs and attested to by the signature of the mechanic who performed the work. You can thus regard logbooks as guides to an airplane's maintenance history rather than iron-clad guarantees of it.

FARs require that when an airplane is repaired or rebuilt following major damage, FAA Form 337 be filled out and forwarded to the FAA's Aircraft Registration Branch in Oklahoma City and that the repair be referenced in the plane's logs, of course. But the log entry may be so terse—"Form 337 filed"—that it will slip past many prospective buyers as something of relative unimportance. And sometimes it is skipped altogether, possibly on the theory that as long as Form 337 went to the FAA, the law has been satisfied.

Occasionally, completely fictitious logbooks surface, usually with a plane that has had a lot of "shade tree" maintenance or perhaps one that has been stolen. In any case, unless you know the plane and the seller, a little amateur detective work may go a long way when you begin your inspection of a used plane and its logs.

Caution is especially necessary when buying a rebuilt airplane, regardless of the quality of the workmanship, because few shops have the jigs to properly realign a bent fuselage, which may result in the wings and/or tail surfaces being slightly out of rig. Rebuilts may contain other flaws, including undetected hairline cracks in fittings or crash-induced conditions that have yet to manifest themselves in some of the operating systems.

Often, relatively minor, though worrisome, problems turn up in rebuilts—for example, an annoying air leak around a baggage door that increases cabin noise and, in winter, can make the rear seat uncomfortable, or a trim problem at certain power settings. The problem may be psychological, one that comes with the knowledge that this airplane has been wrecked. And you may be reminded of this when over particularly inhospitable terrain or at night with the closest airport fifty miles away. Then you will recall that this engine did suffer a sudden stoppage in an accident, and you will wonder whether or not the crankshaft was properly inspected afterward. Your next thought may be that peace of mind is indeed worth whatever it costs.

Where to Buy   It is probably best to seek the used airplane you want from an established fixed-base operator (FBO) on an airport in your area. You stand small chance of finding a big bargain this way—his overhead costs are high, and he has to make a profit—but if he makes any promises or guarantees, you will know where to find him, and he will invariably feel a greater degree of responsibility to a customer than you can expect to find when dealing with an individual. If you are local, he will hope to have your fuel, maintenance, and hangar business, and it therefore serves his best interest to see to it that you are satisfied.

That is not to say that all FBOs are paragons of virtue; no one has ever heard of one being cited for singing too loudly in church. They are subject to the same human frailties that beset the rest of us. Many will have a "hangar queen" or two that they would very much like to convert to cash and may therefore be tempted to find some persuasive reasons why one of these machines is tailored to your needs. Generally speaking, however, your local FBO, if he has any pride in his business, will deal ethically with you.

This does not diminish your need to inspect thoroughly your intended purchase, its logs, and its registration before you buy, because all too often FBOs fail to do an adequate job of this themselves, relying heavily on the dealers' Aircraft Bluebook to determine the value of a trade-in and its subsequent sale price.

Now, assume that you have arrived at an airport to inspect an airplane that is for sale. It is the type of craft that you have decided is best fitted to your needs, experience, and purse. You do not have time to waste, so you ask the owner how much he wants for it and tell him you would like to see the airframe and engine logs.

When the owner or dealer quotes his price, whatever it is, let him know by the expression on your face that it is more than you expect to pay. This is part of the ritual, a useful part, because if his price is firm he will say so immediately. But if, as is more likely, he has opened with his asking price, and is willing to sell for less if he has to, his response to your pained expression will be a sales talk.

Before studying the logs, walk around the airplane giving it an overall, preliminary check. Look under the belly, the most neglected part as a rule and at the undersides of the horizontal tail. If the plane is fabric-covered, look for "ringworms" and cracks and note the general condition of the finish; if it is all-metal, look for evidence of corrosion, loose rivets (there will usually be a ring of black oxide working from beneath the heads of loose rivets), and any sign of wrinkling or distortion of the skin that could indicate internal damage.

What you are after on this five-minute general inspection is simply an overall impression. Look for signs of leaks (both engine oil and hydraulic) and check the seats and cabin for an indication of the present owner's attitude toward the maintenance of his aircraft. A neat and clean cabin interior is a good sign. It usually means that the engine and operating systems have received similar care.

If your walk-around inspection leaves you favorably impressed, do not reveal it (also part of the ritual) as you study the logs, reading from back to front. That is, start with the most recent entries and read back into time. You are interested in total engine time, time since major and top overhaul, replaced accessories, and so on. Since you are not likely to possess a file of FAA Airworthiness Directives ("AD notes"), you may inquire of the seller if all mandatory AD notes have been complied with; you will ultimately have to leave this determination to a qualified mechanic following your tentative decision to buy.

You may want to make a list of significant maintenance and repair items shown in the logs, including dates performed, in order to visually confirm evidence that such operations were actually and properly carried out.

Then, with the airplane's alleged case history digested, if you still feel that this may be the one you want, it is time to poke into the craft's innards.

Remove all access doors, inspection plates, and fairings that conceal structural attachments. When opening the engine cowling, do not clean anything until you have taken note of any sign of chafing and of oil deposits or other accumulated matter that may offer evidence of fluid leakage or other abnormal conditions that need correction.

If your inspection of the airplane and its logs leaves you favorably impressed, you may ask the owner for a demonstration flight. This will allow you to check the operating systems and see how she flies.

Closing the Deal

You should check radio communications during engine warm-up and taxiing, with navigation lights and beacons turned on. Engine gauges should, of course, be monitored carefully during this time and during your normal pretakeoff run-up. Flight instruments and radio navigation systems ought to be checked in flight.

Courtesy demands that you tell the owner before takeoff exactly what you intend to do with his airplane. Unless it is an aerobatic craft, no fancy didos are justified. You should be able to make a judgment after investigating stall behavior with power off; slow flight; hands-off flight at normal cruise settings; and perhaps a lazy-8 or two.

If you decide to buy, you must have a title search made by one of the bonded firms in the Oklahoma City area that do this regularly. A list of them is available from FAA Aeronautical Center, Aircraft Registration Branch, P.O. Box 25082, Oklahoma City, Oklahoma 73125. Ask for FAA Form 8050-55. Title insurance is available if you want it.

Next, arrange for insurance that protects you from the instant the airplane becomes your property. Too many buyers have lost both money and airplane to delivery flights, theft, and storms because they delayed insuring for only a day or two.

Once assured that the title is clear and insurance effective—and assuming that you have already talked with your banker if the deal is to be financed—you are ready to hand over your check to the seller. He will give you a bill of sale (FAA Form 8050-2). He will also remove his aircraft registration certificate from the airplane, fill out the reverse side, and send it to the FAA Aircraft Registration Branch.

You must fill out your application for aircraft registration (FAA Form 8050-1) and send it, along with the bill of sale and $5, to the Aircraft Registration Branch. The pink copy of your application will serve as temporary registration until the FAA returns your permanent certificate. Most FBOs will have all these forms on hand.

You will also receive from the seller the plane's airframe and engine logs, all service records, the aircraft owner's manual, and service/operating booklets for all radio installations. The plane's Airworthiness Certificate also remains with the aircraft.

There are aircraft listing services that solicit aircraft dealer memberships in a multiple-listing service of used airplanes that is similar to the national real estate listing services. The dealers who participate in this argue that the additional listings they are thus able to offer customers simplify the search for, and purchase of, used aircraft. But this remote inventory primarily serves the dealer rather than the customer. Inevitably, the addition of a middle man and a second dealer raises the price. More important, the customer loses control of the transaction almost from the beginning. The dealer with whom you are dealing will subtly make it clear, before he takes you several hundred miles to see a prospective purchase, that you have agreed to buy if the airplane "is as described." And the description will almost always be accurate—as far as it goes. The trouble is that it is not all that difficult to write a fifty-word description of a turkey to make it sound like an eagle.

So, again, it is best to buy locally, and not necessarily from the biggest operator in your area. Remain in control of the transaction and noncommittal until *you* are ready to make an offer on a machine *you* have appraised to your satisfaction.

2

Inspection Procedures

Most pilots are not aircraft mechanics; and although you as a pilot may follow the same procedures a licensed mechanic would employ to inspect an airplane, you cannot expect to see everything he sees. The clues are there, but visible only to eyes experienced in reading them. Could you tell the difference between a factory weld and a shop weld? Can you judge when an area of corrosion may be safely cleaned and refinished, or an expensive repair is needed?

All of which is to say that it is wise to hire an experienced aircraft mechanic—preferably an AI, and of course one who has no interest in the deal—to inspect the airplane you have tentatively decided upon buying after eliminating others with your own inspections.

A thorough inspection entails a lot of work, but some of the used planes you will consider will not require a thorough check. You will rule out some after studying their logbooks or discovering how they have been used. (Personally, I would never buy an airplane that had been previously owned by a large flying school. Such craft really take a beating.) Others will be eliminated rather quickly by obvious shortcomings, including the need for refinishing.

However, if a new paint job is all a plane needs, that should not turn you off if the price is right. Just remember that the cost of refinishing an all-metal lightplane begins at about $1,500 and that anyone who quotes a lower price is not likely to give you a quality job; there is just too much labor involved. Most of the work is in the cleaning and proper preparation of the surfaces before any paint is applied.

The following aircraft inspection procedures are based upon FAA recommendations (Handbook AC 20-9) and will effectively guide you in appraising the mechanical condition of any light aircraft. I have, of course, cranked in useful tips picked up over the years.

Tools

The tools of inspection are many and varied, from a pocket-sized magnifying glass to a complex X-ray machine. For now, I will list only the tools needed to make a routine inspection:

Small 8- or 10-power magnifying glass
Small mirror (a dentist's angled
  mirror is especially handy)
Flashlight or fluorescent-type droplight
One-inch wire brush
Dull-bladed knife

Round bristle brush and cleaning fluid
Some lintless rags
Small kit of common hand tools, including
  a screwdriver assortment, end
  wrenches, diagonal cutters, etc.

General Rust and Corrosion　　The appearance of rust is well known to everyone. If it has progressed beyond the powder stage to form the characteristic brown crust, you will need an appraisal of the damage by a qualified mechanic. The chrome-moly steel tubing used in aircraft fuselages is highly susceptible to rust, which is why this tubing is usually protected on the outside by zinc chromate paint, whereas the interior of the tubing is either sealed at the factory or treated with linseed oil. Nevertheless, after a few years, water may find its way inside this tubing, especially on floatplanes, and the tubing can rust from the inside while it still appears sound from the outside.

The only way to check for water inside fuselage tubing is to have small holes drilled in the tubing with the airplane resting in a level attitude. If water is present, it will drain from the holes. This test must be performed by, or under the supervision of, an aircraft mechanic. In the case of a floatplane, he will probably feel that it is necessary to cut small pieces from the tubing at certain points in order to make sure that rust has not weakened the structure.

Corrosion of aluminum surfaces is usually caused by damage to, or deterioration of, the protective coating applied to the metal when it was manufactured. Corrosion may also be caused by the paint's coming in contact with an eroding chemical, such as battery acid and insecticides. Contact between two dissimilar metals is still another cause of corrosion. Aircraft based or operated on or near water, especially salt water, are particularly prone to corrosion.

Corrosion is distinguished from staining or residual films by its white or grayish powder or flakes. If pitting is apparent after cleaning off the flakes or powder film, an experienced mechanic should be consulted for a determination of the damage. On aluminum and aluminum-alloy surfaces that have been painted, watch for paint bubbles or blisters. Corrosion can take place under the paint (and people have been known to hide corrosion with paint); therefore, you must be suspicious of any roughness or blisters found on the painted surface of a metal aircraft. The only way to check it out is to clean the suspected area down to bare metal. Naturally, you cannot do this on an airplane you do not own. So, to be on the safe side, you presume corrosion damage to be present under the paint and take that into account in your appraisal of the airplane. No matter how optimistic you are by nature, it pays to be pessimistic when evaluating a used flying machine.

Fuselage　　Examining the interior fuselage through access doors and inspection openings, use your flashlight to look for bent or cracked structural members, rust, and corrosion. Wherever possible, inspect welded joints for cracks, using a magnifying glass. Examine not only the weld itself but the tubing directly adjacent to the weld.

While checking the overall condition of the tubing, keep in mind that if a member has been subjected to compression overload, a definite swelling at either end of the tube can be felt or seen. Sometimes this bulge is not pronounced, but a break in the protective paint coating is usually noticeable.

If the fuselage is of bulkhead and stringer construction, look for cracks in the bulkheads at each stringer attachment.

Carefully examine the flight control system. Inspect the bellcranks for cracks, proper alignment, and security of attachment. Check the control cables for signs of fraying or broken strands, for proper tension (too much tension on one side of a control tends to distort the hinges and elongate the clevis holes, which in turn may lead to control surface flutter in flight), and for proper routing through fairleads and pulleys. Rotate the pulleys to check for flat spots, to provide new bearing surfaces for the cables, and to check for smooth, free operation.

Check the electrical wiring for proper installation and security of attachment. Look for chafing, any possible interference with control cables, and general condition. Inspect the grommets holding the wiring and the wiring insulation.

Examine the baggage compartment for general condition. Inspect the floor for defects and distortion. Check the door hinges, weather seals (air leaks around a baggage door can make rear-seat occupancy uncomfortable in cold weather), and door lock.

Inspect the cabin doors for ease of operation and interior locking method. Most of the older two-placers, and some of the four-placers, such as the Piper Tri-Pacer and even the Comanche, have interior door-latching systems that are pure abominations.

Cabin

Employing your flashlight, check under the instrument panel for loose wires and leaks in the instrument lines. Check operation of the controls for freedom of movement and full travel. Check the fuel selector valve for leaks, freedom of movement, and proper operation. It should click solidly into each position. Also check the primer for leaks and proper operation.

Lift the carpet and inspect around the rudder and brake pedals for signs of hydraulic leaks.

Inspect the electric wire bundles for general condition, chafing, and proper routing. Examine the connections at terminals, junction boxes, cannon plugs, and clips for looseness and obvious defects. Check the condition and operation of circuit breakers, fuses, and switches.

Inspect the instrument panel for freedom of movement and its shock mounts for signs of deterioration. The panel should not come in contact with any part of the aircraft structure or any line or component rigidly attached to the airframe.

Check the seat adjustment mechanisms, along with seat-belt and shoulder-harness attach points.

Inspect the cabin heating and ventilating system for leakage and the condition of units, lines, and fittings. Check system operation by moving the controls. This check is best deferred, of course, until you fly the airplane, assuming that other factors do not eliminate it from consideration before you reach that point.

Carefully inspect all windows and the windshield for cracks and crazing. Most cracks start from the edges of Plexiglas and are often caused by an insufficient gap between window and frame to allow for expansion of the plastic caused by high temperatures.

Engine Compartment

With the fuel selector and boost pump on, inspect the fuel lines and connections for leaks, cracks, kinks, chafing, and security of mounting. Examine hoses and clamps.

Inspect the carburetor for security of attachment, and look for excessive wear at throttle shaft, link assemblies, and hot-air butterfly shaft bearing points, any one of which can affect the fuel–air mixture, resulting in erratic engine operation. Inspect for leaks due to damaged gaskets and loose or damaged fuel-line fittings. Assure that the carburetor heater is properly secured and heater doors operate throughout their full range.

Examine the intake manifolds for general condition, cracks, kinks, and evidence of leakage. Air leaks are found by mechanics by squirting a little gasoline around intake manifold connections with the engine idling. This results in a temporary increase in engine rpms if the connections are not airtight.

If this is a dry-sump engine, inspect the oil tank for evidence of cracks or oil leaks, especially around welded seams and fittings. Also check the oil tank for chafing at the adjustable retainer straps and for security of attachment. Oil lines and hoses, along with their connectors, should also be examined for condition and proper clamp tension.

On wet-sump engines, about all you can do is clean the crankcase and look for cracks, particularly at attaching studs. Later, if you are on the verge of buying such a machine, the mechanic you hire for the final, thorough check will remove the oil-sump plug and inspect for foreign particles. The presence of metal particles usually indicates an internal engine-component failure and requires engine disassembly for internal inspection.

Check other engine accessories, such as alternator, magnetos, and starter for general appearance, and examine ignition wiring and connections.

You should inspect the exhaust system as thoroughly as you can, because any leak can be dangerous. Another of the things your mechanic will do on the final before-the-sale inspection is remove the heater shroud from the exhaust system to complete this check.

20

Although it is legal for you to do so, there is not much point in bothering to remove a spark plug or two to check their condition, because your mechanic will do this when he runs a compression check on each cylinder.

You can inspect the cylinders for cracks or broken cooling fins, and check the baffles for security, holes, cracks, and proper fit around the cylinders. Also inspect all air entrances and exits for deformities that might obstruct the airflow. Using your flashlight, look through the nose cowling and check for gaps between the top cowling and engine baffles. Since most air-cooled engines require pressurized air for cooling, any leak around or through the baffles causes a pressure drop that reduces the cooling efficiency of the engine.

If the airplane you are inspecting has cowl flaps, determine that they are in good operating condition and that the hinges are not excessively worn. Proper operation of the cowl flaps is vital to holding cylinder-head temperatures within safe limits.

Clean the entire engine mount structure, and examine it with a magnifying glass, especially at welds, for evidence of cracks. Some engine mounts are heat-treated and cannot be repaired by welding unless normalized and retreated to their original strength values. Here again, your mechanic's practiced eye is valuable.

Check the condition of the firewall behind the engine, especially for oil or fuel saturation, since this can be a serious fire hazard.

Check the hydraulic reservoir for general condition, security of attachment, and proper fluid level. Examine the pressure accumulator for obvious defects. Check the pumps for security of mounting and condition. Inspect the bypass and relief valves for leaks, and assure that the lines are properly secured and free from leaks, kinks, cracks, and chafing. No wire carrying an electrical charge should ever be allowed to come in direct contact with hydraulic lines.

Examine the battery installation for sign of corrosion and security of attachment. Inspect the vents and overflow lines for condition and proper routing. These lines should be routed to prevent overflowing electrolyte from contacting and corroding the adjacent structure. The battery box should be protected with acid-proof paint.

Landing Gear (Fixed)

There are numerous types of landing gears, but since the inspection procedures for them are similar, there is no need to discuss them separately. Begin with the tires, and remember that wheel pants (or "speed fairings," as the new crowd likes to call them) may hide a lot of defects. This is another item you may leave to the mechanic you hire for the final, presale inspection, because he will pull the wheels anyway to check brakes and wheel bearings. And if there is uneven tire wear, he can tell from the pattern of wear what the cause is.

Oil and gasoline cause rapid deterioration of rubber in a tire. An airplane should not be parked in a puddle of oil, and since the main gear wheels are 21 usually beneath the engines in a twin-engined craft, the tires should be protected when such craft are parked for long periods of time if oil leaks are present.

You can inspect hydraulic brake lines and, if the wheel is not covered, check for leakage around the inside wheel hub. When you fly the airplane, you may note sponginess in the brake pedals; that usually indicates air in the system.

When shock cords are used as shock absorbers, inspect them for general condition, cleanliness, and fraying. Shock cords consist of many rubber strands covered with a protective cloth cover, and accumulations of gasoline or oil will deteriorate them. The Piper Tri-Pacer employs shock cords (or "shock rings," as they are sometimes called), as do many of the older two-place aircraft.

The spring-steel-type gear legs of the Cessnas and the later steel-tube gear legs of four-place Cessnas act as shock absorbers and require almost no maintenance. But you should check for cracks in the area where the attachment brackets are riveted to the fuselage and attach to the unit.

Inspect oleo-type shock absorbers for cleanliness, leaks, cracks, and possible bottoming of the pistons. Clean and check all bolts and fittings.

Clean and carefully examine the landing-gear attachment fittings at the fuselage, including bolt holes that may have become elongated or torn as a result of an unusually hard landing. When an aircraft is of all-metal construction, overloads are often evidenced by wrinkling of the skin in areas surrounding the points of landing-gear attachment.

Landing Gear (Retractable)   When inspecting retractable landing gears, particular attention should be given to the locking mechanisms, drag struts, shock struts, stops, linkages, and alignment. Examine fairing doors for satisfactory operation, proper rigging, and loose or broken hinges.

Check the nose gear and main gear up-latches for general condition and proper operation. Inspect the down-lock mechanism and power source for general condition.

Inspect the retracting and extending mechanisms for general condition, including security of attachment. Determine that the actuating cylinders, sprockets, universals, and chain or drive gears are in good condition; you will have to refer to the manufacturer's recommended maximum tolerances in order to pin down the permissible wear.

Inspect the aircraft structure to which the landing gear is attached for distortion, cracks, and general condition. Be sure that all bolts and rivets are intact and secure. The only way I know of to be absolutely certain of a bolt's condition is to back it out, thoroughly clean it, and examine it with a magnifying glass. Cracks in bolts are most often found in the shank just below the head.

If the gear is electrically operated, inspect the electric motors for security of attachment, cleanliness, and any obvious defects. Assure that the wiring is in good condition and properly routed and secured to prevent interference with movable members. Determine that protective rubber or plastic caps are properly installed over all wire terminals requiring such protection.

"If the landing gear is hydraulically operated, inspect all actuators for general condition, leakage, and operation throughout their full range of travel." This is the way the FAA says it, but in order to do this you are going to have to either jack up the airplane or fly it. You cannot exercise the gear with the airplane resting upon it. And since jacking more than one wheel at a time is a ticklish proposition best left to qualified aircraft mechanics, the only operational test you can give the retractable landing gear is in flight. But you can inspect for leaks and make certain that the lines are free from chafing and are securely attached.

Wings   Examine the wings' fabric or metal skin, as the case may be, paying particular attention to the upper surfaces if the wing is fabric-covered. A beat-up leading edge subtracts from the plane's performance, and any sign of distortion or wrinkle in the surfaces indicates internal damage. Grasp each wingtip in turn and gently rock the airplane; this, too, may reveal internal damage, either through sound or feel.

With the fairings off and all access doors and inspection plates open, use your flashlight (and mirror if needed) to examine the wings' interiors. Every wing should be dry and clean inside. Varnish on wood components should be shiny and new-looking. Examine the wing ribs, compression members, drag wires, and, if the wing is fabric-covered, the method of fabric attachment to the wing ribs. If this is by means of rib-lacing cords (the most common method), carefully inspect these cords for condition; if someone has been careless enough to park the airplane with an inspection plate open, mud-dauber nests or even mice could be present. Mice love rib-stitching cord. And while on the subject of our furry friends consuming airplanes, never park a fabric-covered plane in a field with cattle; cows can eat a lot of fabric overnight.

If the wings are metal-framed, inspect for cracks, distortion, and signs of corrosion.

Examine control-system bellcranks for cracks, proper alignment, and security of attachment. Check control cables for fraying, wear, and proper routing through fairleads and pulleys.

Determine that wing attachment fittings are not distorted, cracked, or damaged in any way and that the bolt holes have not become elongated.

If you are inspecting a biplane, pay particular attention to the interwing bracing wires (flying and landing wires) to make sure that there are a sufficient number of threads holding in the adjusting terminals. Count the threads showing on the male fitting. If more than three threads show, the connection is not satisfactory. Inspect the fittings where they attach to the wing structure for distortion, cracks, and other defects. Inspect clevises for wear, cracks, and thread condition.

23

Next, examine the movable surfaces (ailerons, flaps, and trim tabs) for damage and obvious defects. Check for loose rivets, distortion, and general condition. Inspect the hinges and control horns for security of attachment, excessive wear, breaks, and bends.

Returning to the inside of the wings, check the fuel tanks and fuel lines for security of attachment and any sign of leakage. Then trace all electrical wiring in the wings looking for chafing, possible interference with control action, security of attachment, and condition of insulation. Remember, electrical wiring should never come in contact with a fuel cell or hydraulic line.

If you are inspecting a strut-braced monoplane, check the attachment fittings at wing and fuselage. Never step on a lift strut. Bent lift struts almost always have to be replaced; repair is seldom possible.

Empennage

Inspect the fixed tail surfaces for damage; loose rivets, screws, or bolts; condition of covering and finish; and condition of the ribs and stabilizer spars at points of attachment. The movable control surfaces should be similarly examined, especially the undersides of the horizontal stabilizer and elevators, which are subject to damage from rocks and debris thrown back by the propeller and wheels. Inspect the hinges and horns for security of attachment, breaks, or bends. Examine the hinges for loose or worn pins.

Inspect the external bracing attachment fittings for distortion, cracks, and security of attachment. Similarly examine struts and brace wires, and determine that clevises are free of cracks and damaged threads. Bracing must not be slack, which can cause flutter, nor should there be excessive tension, which might distort or damage fittings or attachments.

Inspect the control cables and bolts for wear at horns or bellcranks. Inspect the trim-adjustment mechanism for excessive looseness.

Propeller

Inspect metal propeller blades for corrosion, cracks, nicks, and scratches, particularly on the leading edge of each blade from the tip inboard for approximately eight inches. Nicks and scratches set up concentrations of stress which can exceed the strength of the blade material; the result will be a crack and failure of the blade.

Wood or composition blades should be inspected for condition of metal tipping and leading-edge strips. Check for loose rivets or screws, separation of soldered joints, and other signs of creeping and looseness of the metal tipping. Check for lamination separation, especially between the metal leading edge and cap, and the condition of fabric sheathing. Inspect the tip for cracks by grasping with your hand and slightly twisting and bending the tip backward and forward. A fine line appearing in the fabric or plastic will indicate a crack in the wood.

24

Assure yourself that the tip drain holes are open. These holes allow the centrifugal force of the revolving prop to dissipate moisture.

If inspecting other than a fixed-pitch propeller, make certain that the blades are installed in the hub satisfactorily and are properly safetied. The wood close to the metal sleeve of wood blades should be examined for cracks extending outward on the blade.

Inspect the hub for corrosion, cracks, oil leaks, and security of attachment, and make sure that the retainer bolts are properly safetied.

Inspect the propeller control system for security of attachment, oil leaks, and condition of wiring. Examine the tubing for kinks and chafing. The control system may incorporate a full feathering system, including relays, solenoids, governors or control valves, and distributors, all of which may be a bit foreign to you. But you can recognize an oil leak, chafing, and unsafetied nuts, and leave the final inspection to a qualified mechanic if the plane you tentatively decide to buy has a full feathering system. And since the screws holding the propeller spinner are sometimes hard to back out with simple hand tools, you may choose to skip this operation entirely if you intend to hire a mechanic to back up your decision.

As mentioned in the first chapter, such items as engine gauges, flight instruments, position lights, anticollision beacons, and radios are things you will check operationally during a demonstration flight.

Does all this seem like a lot of trouble? Well, consider this: you can perform the above-listed operations in about an hour, perhaps an hour and a half. If a given machine is below par, you probably will discover that rather quickly and invest much less time than that. Eventually, you may have five or six hours invested in inspections before you find the airplane you think you want and call in an AI to firm up your decision. Altogether, that is not really much of an expenditure for safety, the protection of a significant investment, and your peace of mind.

3

Used Two-Place Airplanes

Chances are, you learned to fly in a two-place, fixed-gear airplane and are therefore familiar with their limitations. However, since these were school airplanes, you may not have given much thought to their depreciation, maintenance, and operating costs. In any case, it should be obvious that the "minimum" airplane generates minimum costs. Well, usually.

The problem is that if you are seeking the lowest-cost flying, primarily for pleasure in your spare time, you may be attracted to one of the older fabric-covered airplanes. Such machines may be owned and operated very cheaply, or they can be expensive headaches. It all depends on the fabric covering.

It currently costs about $3,500 to have a J-3 Cub or Aeronca Champ re-covered. Therefore, as a general rule, you would probably be well advised to pass up the rag-wings—unless you are willing to expend the considerable labor involved in re-covering such an airplane yourself. The materials alone will cost between $400 and $800, depending upon the cover-and-finish system selected.

This is certainly worthy of consideration by many pilots and aircraft owners, because a rag-wing that clearly needs re-covering should be priced accordingly. It may not be the easiest way to make $3,000 in your spare time, but it is one way.

As often as not, it is the only way to be sure that the job is properly done. All re-cover jobs look good initially; the peeling and cracking starts a year or so later if incompatible solvent systems were used or other errors or cost-cutting methods were employed in the finishing.

That is not to say that you cannot find a good fabric-covered airplane in the used aircraft market; the problem is differentiating between what is good and what merely looks good. The airframe log is a help if it is accurate. It is better if you know the airplane, and best if you know the mechanic who covered and finished it.

I will discuss the two-placers in alphabetical order, listing all that are to be found in today's used market with some regularity.

Re-covering your "rag-wing" yourself saves at least 75 percent of the cost and insures a proper job. *Courtesy of Razorback Fabrics, Inc.*

The Aeronca Champion series appeared in 1945 and evolved from the Army's L-3 liaison plane of World War II. The Model 7AC, the first of the series, was available with a Continental, Lycoming, or Franklin engine of 65 hp and was produced in some numbers to fill the needs of civilian operators who had been without new training planes since the war's beginning.

The Champion Model 7BCM followed in 1947, fitted with the 85-hp Continental. A year later, the 7CCM was announced, featuring a larger fin and some minor structural changes. Then, through 1949 and 1950 the Model 7DC was produced, equipped with the Continental C85-8F (flange-type crankshaft for metal prop).

All these craft have wood spars with aluminum wing ribs. The fuselage is welded steel tubing, and the entire aircraft structure is fabric-covered. Seating is tandem. None of this series was originally equipped with starter or generator, and these accessories cannot be installed without going to the C85-12 engine. However, hand-propping the small Continentals is easy and, as Bill Lear once pointed out, "You'll never have to service, repair, or maintain anything you leave out."

The Aeronca Champs ("Airknockers" to the old hands) have never presented any special maintenance problems. These are honest little craft, with no bad flight characteristics. They are a tad less gentle than the J-3 Cub because of a slightly higher wing-loading. Something over 7,000 were built, and a surprising number are still around. Fuel consumption will average about 4.5 gallons per hour.

Aeroncas* Champion Models 7AC, 7BCM, 7CCM, and 7DC

Aeronca Champion, Model 7DC

Wing span	35 ft, 2 in	Maximum speed	102 mph (89 kt)
Length	21 ft, 6 in	Cruising speed	92 mph (80 kt)
Empty weight	809 lb	Stalling speed	44 mph (38 kt)
Gross weight	1,300 lb	Initial climb	750 ft/min
Useful load	491 lb	Service ceiling	14,500 ft
Wing loading	7.63 lb/sq ft	Range (18.5 gal)	360 sm (statute miles)
Power loading	15.3 lb/hp		

*The early fifties saw a severe drop in new airplane sales—a total of 2,477 civil aircraft of all kinds were built in 1951—and Aeronca production stopped in that year. The Champion design, however, was too useful to die, and so modified versions reappeared in 1955, produced by the Champion Aircraft Company of Osceola, Wisconsin. In 1970, this firm became the Champion Division of the Bellanca Aircraft Corporation. These machines will be listed under *Champion*.

The Aeronca Champs are honest little craft, with no special maintenance problems.

Aeronca Super Chief, Model 11AC

The Aeronca Chief was a 50-hp pre–World War II craft with side-by-side seating and wood-framed wings. After the war, the Super Chief appeared in the same configuration, but with the A65 Continental engine. Never as popular as the Champs, the Super Chief was built in fewer numbers and is relatively rare today.

Beechcraft Sport, Model 19

The 150-hp Beech Musketeer Sport was introduced in 1965, to join the Model 23 four-place Musketeers that first appeared in 1962. The Sport may be equipped with a rear seat, although with four aboard you will have to go with fuel tanks half full and very little baggage. This airplane is all metal, the fuselage employing bulkheads and the skin providing its own stringers via ninety-degree bends at each splice. The wing has a single, heavy spar with ribs cut from sheets of aluminum honeycomb sandwich, to which the skin is chemically bonded.

The Sport's cabin is roomy and relatively quiet, with the baggage area accessible in flight. Upholstery is vinyl, and the Narco Mark 8 Nav/Comm system is standard equipment. This airplane may have either a 60-gal or 40-gal fuel capacity, and some were built with 15-gal tanks in each wing. The engine is the Lycoming O-320-E2C. Beech's suggested selling price in 1969 was $15,450.

An aerobatic version, introduced in 1968, was called the Sport III; but this craft must be regarded as the least aerobatic of all the standard production airplanes licensed as "aerobatic" by the manufacturers. Two hands are needed on the wheel in order to perform a good inside loop, because of heavy stabilator forces, while a third hand is needed for power management. However, any roll maneuver is delightful because of the very effective ailerons.

Beechcraft Sport 150, Model 19.

Beechcraft Model 77, an all-new two-placer with 115 hp, entered production in 1978.

The Sport's landing gear requires little maintenance. The three gear legs are identical, the shocks consisting of rubber biscuits in compression.

Beechcraft Sport, Model 19

Wing span	32 ft, 9 in	Baggage capacity	340 lb
Length	25 ft, 7.5 in	Maximum speed	140 mph (124 kt)
Height	8 ft, 2.5 in	Cruising speed	131 mph (114 kt)
Empty weight	1,374 lb	Stalling speed	55 mph (48 kt)
Gross weight	2,250 lb	Initial climb	700 ft/min
Useful load	876 lb	Service ceiling	11,100 ft
Wing loading	15.14 lb/sq ft	Range (60 gal)	767 sm
Power loading	15 lb/hp		

Cessna 120 and 140

Maybe it is nostalgia—or maybe just an imperfect memory. Whatever, it seems to me now that the Cessna 140s I remember were near-ideal little airplanes. One thing cannot be denied: with less horsepower and lower operating costs, a good 120 or 140 can crowd modern Cessna 150s in performance—and is a lot more fun to fly. True, the older craft are not as pretty or as comfortable and require a little more effort to land properly; but they are as trouble-free as their modern counterparts (except for those with fabric wings that need re-covering), and depreciation has long since ceased to be a factor, because a 120 or 140 in top condition will bring more in the used market now than it cost new.

The 120 and 140 represent two versions of the same airframe. The 120 is the economy model, without an electrical system, starter, or flaps. Both were originally powered with the C85 Continental, except for about 500 metal-winged 140s that were given the C90 engine. The 140s had an extra

The Cessna 140, produced from 1946 to 1951, brings more in today's used aircraft market than it sold for when new.

window on each side, a plusher cabin, and more instruments. But a lot of 120s were modified by their owners to look like 140s and even given the C85-12 engine with generator and starter. That would make a 120 close enough to a 140 to justify calling it a 140, because the flaps on the true 140 are so small and generally ineffective that you can land without them and hardly tell the difference.

These are simple airplanes, with gravity-fed fuel from two 12.5-gal wing tanks, and rather snug side-by-side seating. Fuel consumption will be between 4 and 6 gal/h.

These craft will require between 600 and 700 ft for takeoff with no wind. They will begin flying at slightly over 40 mph indicated, and will climb out at 600 ft/min showing 85 mph. Stalls are gentle but definitely more pronounced than stalls in the 150, with some warning buffeting prior to the break. If you land the 140 as you properly do all airplanes—that is, cut power in the downwind leg opposite your touchdown point and bring it to a full stall about a foot above the runway—then 70 mph indicated is a good gliding speed through base leg into final, and your speed, adjusted of course with the control wheel, should be down to about 55 mph indicated when you begin your flare at about 6 ft or so. Sure, it takes practice.

In sum, perhaps the best of the older two-placers.

Cessna 140 (90 hp)

Wing span	33 ft, 4 in	Baggage capacity	54 lb
Length	21 ft, 6 in	Maximum speed	125 mph (109 kt)
Height	6 ft, 3 in	Cruising speed	105 mph (91 kt)
Empty weight	890 lb	Stalling speed	45 mph (39 kt)
Gross weight	1,450 lb	Initial climb	680 ft/min
Useful load	560 lb	Service ceiling	15,500 ft
Wing loading	9.1 lb/sq ft	Range (25 gal)	450 sm
Power loading	17.1 lb/hp		

Cessna Model 150 and Aerobat

The Cessna 150 entered the market late in 1958, almost eight years after the last 140A was built. Cessna did not produce a two-place airplane during those lean years of the fifties, but the Cessna 172 had appeared in 1956, and its success suggested that Cessna's design philosophy for light aircraft had, for the first time, put the company in a position to challenge Piper's long-time dominance of this market. Clearly, a new Cessna two-place trainer and sport plane was needed; and since the trigear, four-place 172 had been so well received, Cessna, seeing no reason to tamper with success, introduced the new 150 as a scaled-down version of the 172.

It was squarely on target. Fitted with the Continental 0-200 engine of 100 hp, the Cessna 150 soon became the most popular sport/trainer in the Free World, and by 1969, 61 percent of all flight training hours were flown in

Cessnas.

The Cessna 150 Aerobat is certified
for limited aerobatics.
Pictured is the 1974 model.

The Cessna 150 was introduced in
1959. Shown here is the 1968 model.

31

The 150 has always been offered in three versions, the Standard, Trainer, and Commuter, the difference being a matter of equipment, mostly radios.

The 150 has changed some over the years. The big rear window was added in 1964; doors were enlarged and swept rudder and bigger tires added in 1966; the conical-camber wingtips first appeared on the 1970 model; in 1971 the 150 received the tubular steel landing-gear legs, a new nose plate with landing light, and an extended propeller shaft, along with a new dorsal fin. The paint jobs, of course, were changed from year to year and the wheel pants reshaped as a matter of eye appeal, while minor improvements accrued in the cabin from year to year. The 1973 model has lower seats for more headroom, and a redesigned instrument panel with new control wheels. In 1974 the Aerobat model was given a propeller possessing a Clark Y airfoil to improve performance, and this feature was added to the 150s the following year, along with increased rudder and fin area.

The Aerobat version, approved for limited aerobatics, was announced in 1970, and its special equipment includes quick-release door mechanisms, seats with removable cushions to accommodate parachutes, quick-release lap and shoulder belts, G-meter, and a distinctive paint job. It is stressed for 6 Gs positive and 3 Gs negative flight loads.

The 150s are a little lighter on the controls than the Piper Cherokee trainers and, in my opinion, land better because you seem to have more control through those final 3 or 4 ft. Stalls are hardly worth mentioning. With power off and no flaps, the 150 just mushes along with the wheel all the way back and the airspeed needle bouncing somewhere around 45 and 50 mph. With flaps down, it will buffet gently and dip its nose somewhere below 45 mph indicated; you cannot tell exactly, because the needle is bouncing around, and it probably is not very accurate anyway under these conditions. More like old times is stalling this airplane out of a 30-degree bank with flaps. The break is quite clean, and the buffeting pronounced, with the break coming at about 60 mph or a mite under. The airplane responds immediately to normal recovery technique.

The 1977 Cessna Commuter II.

Cessna 150 and Aerobat

	1972 Model 150	**1977 Model 150**
Wing span	32 ft, 8.5 in	33 ft, 2 in
Length	23 ft, 9 in	23 ft, 11 in
Empty weight	1,000 lb	1,111 lb
Gross weight	1,600 lb	1,600 lb
Useful load	600 lb	489 lb
Wing loading	10.2 lb/sq ft	10 lb/sq ft
Power loading	16 lb/hp	16 lb/hp
Baggage capacity	120 lb	120 lb
Maximum speed	122 mph (106 kt)	125 mph (109 kt)
Cruising speed	117 mph (103 kt)	122 mph (106 kt)
Stalling speed	48 mph (42 kt)	48 mph (42 kt)
Initial climb	670 ft/min	670 ft/min
Service ceiling	12,650 ft	14,000 ft
Range (22.5 gal)	475 sm	390 sm

In April 1977, Cessna announced that production would stop on the Model 150 after a nineteen-year production run of almost 24,000 of the venerable little sport/trainers. Its follow-on would be the 1978 Cessna 152, the first deliveries of which began in May 1977. An Aerobat version of the 152 appeared at the same time. The new 152 is essentially a 150 fitted with the Lycoming O-235-L2C engine of 110 hp.

The obvious reason for the change is that the O-235-L2C burns 100-octane (low-lead) fuel, and a lot of people apparently expect 80 octane to disappear permanently one day in the not-too-distant future as it did temporarily in the mid-1970s. Whether or not it will disappear is not the point; if a lot of pilots fear that it will, that would be reason enough for the engine change. True, you can burn 100 octane in an engine rated for 80 octane, but if you are one of those who did so when the U.S. oil cartel cut off your 80-octane supply so capriciously, you know the added maintenance costs that were forced on you for spark-plug and valve work, along with more frequent oil changes.

So, Cessna heeded the voices crying in the aeronautical wilderness and selected a high-compression version of an engine that has been around even longer than the one it replaced. The first O-235s were fitted to the Piper Super Cruiser (PA-12) of 1946. It has powered Citabrias and Yankees and a lot of other two-placers in the meantime.

The 152 has a one-piece, easily removable cowling, to which the engine baffles are attached for quick access to the engine. It also has a 28-v electrical system. The first 152s were priced at $14,950 for the standard model, $17,995 for the Model 152 II, and $19,500 for the 152 Aerobat. Conical wingtips and wheel pants were extra-cost items.

Cessna Model 152

Wing span	33 ft, 2 in	Baggage capacity	120 lb
Length	24 ft, 1 in	Maximum speed	126 mph (110 kt)
Height	8 ft, 6 in	Cruising speed	123 mph (107 kt)
Empty weight	1,081 lb	Stalling speed	48 mph (43 kt)
Gross weight	1,670 lb	Initial climb	715 ft/min
Useful load	598 lb	Service ceiling	14,700 ft
Wing loading	10.5 lb/sq ft	Range (24.5 gal)	400 sm
Power loading	15.2 lb/hp		

The Champion Traveler 7EC appeared in 1955 as a 90-hp version of the earlier Aeronca 7DC. The Tri-Traveler, with tricycle gear, was also offered in several models, including the Tri-Con, Sky-Trac, DXer, and the Challenger. The DXer was fitted with a 135-hp Lycoming as the Model 7HC, and the Challenger Model 7GCB was powered with an O-320 Lycoming of 150 hp.

All have tandem seating and are metal-framed with fabric covering, and though the 90-hp models are a little heavier than the last Aeroncas, they are slightly faster and have larger fuel capacities.

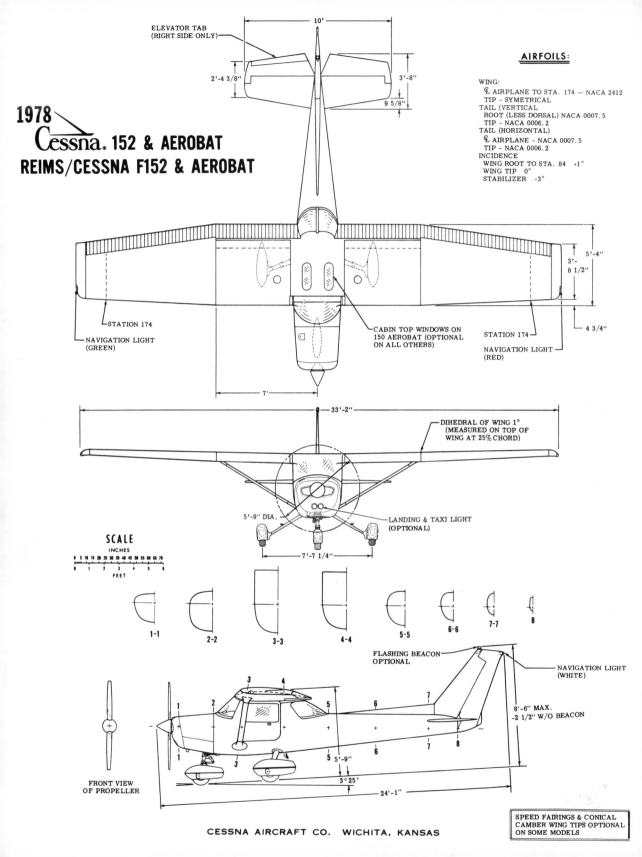

ELEVATOR TAB
(RIGHT SIDE ONLY)

10'

2'-4 3/8"

3'-8"

9 5/8"

1978
Cessna. 152 & AEROBAT
REIMS/CESSNA F152 & AEROBAT

AIRFOILS:

WING:
℄ AIRPLANE TO STA. 174 — NACA 2412
TIP - SYMETRICAL
TAIL (VERTICAL
ROOT (LESS DORSAL) NACA 0007.5
TIP - NACA 0006.2
TAIL (HORIZONTAL)
℄ AIRPLANE - NACA 0007.5
TIP - NACA 0006.2
INCIDENCE
WING ROOT TO STA. 84 +1°
WING TIP 0°
STABILIZER -3°

STATION 174

NAVIGATION LIGHT
(GREEN)

CABIN TOP WINDOWS ON
150 AEROBAT (OPTIONAL
ON ALL OTHERS)

STATION 174

NAVIGATION LIGHT
(RED)

5'-4"

3'-8 1/2"

4 3/4"

7'

33'-2"

DIHEDRAL OF WING 1°
(MEASURED ON TOP OF
WING AT 25% CHORD)

5'-9" DIA.

LANDING & TAXI LIGHT
(OPTIONAL)

7'-7 1/4"

SCALE
INCHES
0 5 10 15 20 25 30 35 40 45 50 55 60 65 70
0 1 2 3 4 5 6
FEET

1-1   2-2   3-3   4-4   5-5   6-6   7-7   8

FLASHING BEACON
OPTIONAL

NAVIGATION LIGHT
(WHITE)

3   4

1   2

5   6   7

5'-9"

3°25'

8'-6" MAX.
-2 1/2" W/O BEACON

FRONT VIEW
OF PROPELLER

24'-1"

SPEED FAIRINGS & CONICAL
CAMBER WING TIPS OPTIONAL
ON SOME MODELS

CESSNA AIRCRAFT CO. WICHITA, KANSAS

Actually, Champion also offered a two-place twin-engine craft called the Lancer (Model 402), powered with two Continental O-200 engines of 100 hp each, during the early sixties, but few were sold, and I have not seen one in the used market for a long time. The Lancer, by the way, was high-winged and fabric-covered.

Champion Tri-Traveler 7FC

Wing span	33 ft, 5 in	Baggage capacity	50 lb
Length	21 ft, 8 in	Maximum speed	135 mph (117 kt)
Height	8 ft, 8 in	Cruising speed	108 mph (94 kt)
Empty weight	968 lb	Stalling speed	40 mph (35 kt)
Gross weight	1,500 lb	Initial climb	900 ft/min
Useful load	532 lb	Service ceiling	14,000 ft
Wing loading	8.8 lb/sq ft	Range (26 gal)	500 sm
Power loading	16.5 lb/hp		

The Champion trigear series produced during the 1950s were fitted with engines ranging from 90 hp to 150 hp.

The Citabria, produced by the Champion Division of Bellanca, has been in production since 1964 with several engine options.

35

**Champion
Citabria,
Models 7ELA,
7ECA, 7GCAA,
7KCAB, and
7GCBC**

The Citabrias do resemble the original Aeroncas but actually represent a new design that was introduced in 1964. The first one, Model 7ELA, was fitted with the Continental 0-200 engine of 100 hp, the same engine that powers the Cessna 150; but relatively few of these were built before the 7ECA came along equipped with the Lycoming O-235, rated at 115 hp.

The Citabrias are of the same general configuration as the earlier Champions and Aeroncas, but tandem seating, conventional landing gear, and a fabric-covered (Ceconite) metal structure. All are approved for limited aerobatics. If you doubt that, just spell *Citabria* backward.

In 1966, Champion added the 150-hp Citabria, 7GCAA, powered with the Lycoming O-320-A2B engine. Later, the 7KCAB appeared fitted with the IO-320-E2A featuring fuel injection. The 7GCBC has the O-320-A2B Lyc, flaps, and a wing span one foot greater. Late model Citabrias all feature a spring-steel landing gear.

The Citabrias are better aerobatic airplanes than the Cessna Aerobats, even with the same horsepower; and with 150 hp, the Citabria is far more versatile in this category than the Cessna Aerobat or Beechcraft Sport. Control pressures are a bit heavy, about like those of the Stearman biplane, especially in roll maneuvers. In normal flight regimes, however, these craft have a nice feel, a good balance between responsiveness and stability.

After Champion Aircraft became the Champion Division of Bellanca in 1970, the company tried to revive the Aeronca 7AC design by fitting it with a 60-hp two-cylinder Franklin engine (2A 120-B) and marketed it with a base sticker price of $4,995; but few were sold and production soon stopped. I have never seen one offered in the used market.

Champion Citabria

	Model 7ECA	Model 7KCAB
Wing span	33 ft, 5 in	33 ft, 5 in
Length	22 ft, 7 in	22 ft, 7 in
Height	7 ft	7 ft
Empty weight	1,034 lb	1,118 lb
Gross weight	1,650 lb	1,650 lb
Useful load	616 lb	532 lb
Wing loading	10 lb/sq ft	10 lb/sq ft
Power loading	14.3 lb/hp	11 lb/hp
Baggage capacity	100 lb	100 lb
Maximum speed	119 mph (103 kt)	132 mph (113 kt)
Cruising speed	112 mph (97 kt)	125 mph (109 kt)
Stalling speed	51 mph (45 kt)	51 mph (45 kt)
Initial climb	725 ft/min	1,120 ft/min
Service ceiling	12,000 ft	17,000 ft
Range (36 gal)	690 sm	525 sm

The Champion Decathlon model is essentially a 150-hp Citabria with a constant-speed propeller and special wing, a wing designed primarily for advanced aerobatics. This wing employs a nearly symmetrical airfoil section and has a shorter span with wider chord than the Citabria's wing. Full inverted engine systems and an airframe stressed for 6 G positive and 5 G negative flight loads mark the Decathlon as a truly advanced aerobatic machine. Also, its beefed-up control cables, working on ball-bearing mounted pulleys, significantly lighten control pressures. And although this airplane cannot be considered in the same class with the unlimited akro craft, such as the Pitts, Great Lakes, and Jungmeister, it offers full electrical and avionic systems, along with a comfortable cabin environment that the unlimited aerobatic biplanes cannot match for cross-country and night flying and is therefore a more practical flying machine for all except national and world competitions. Decathlon construction is similar to that of the Citabrias, metal-framed and fabric-covered. It is a fun machine possessing a lot of utility and, of course, more aerobatic potential than most pilots have the skill to exploit.

Champion Decathlon 8KCAB

The Champion Scout is a Citabria with a longer wing and the 180-hp Lycoming O-360-C2E engine. Earlier 7GCBC Citabrias with 150-hp Lycomings are sometimes called Scouts, since they have the longer wing. The 8GCBC has oversize tires, a bigger vertical fin, and Hoerner wingtips. It is a utility craft, intended for mountain and bush operations; it is supposed to earn its keep. Its performance is a bit underwhelming for its power; but it will get into and out of small fields and high-altitude fields with a load. Produced in limited numbers, 8GCBCs first appeared in 1974 and are not plentiful in the used market.

Champion Scout 8GCBC

Champion Decathlon 8KCAB and Scout 8GCBC

	Decathlon 8KCAB	Scout 8GCBC
Wing span	32 ft	36 ft
Length	22 ft, 11 in	23 ft
Height	7 ft, 9 in	7 ft
Empty weight	1,275 lb	1,315 lb
Gross weight	1,800 lb	2,150 lb
Useful load	525 lb	835 lb
Maximum speed	144 mph (126 kt)	135 mph (117 kt)
Cruising speed	140 mph (122 kt)	125 mph (109 kt)
Stalling speed	53 mph (47 kt)	53 mph (47 kt)
Initial climb	1,025 ft/min	1,000 ft/min
Service ceiling	16,000 ft	17,500 ft
Range	620 sm (40 gal)	375 sm (35 gal)

The Decathlon is essentially a 150-hp Citabria with constant-speed propeller and a special wing designed for advanced aerobatics.

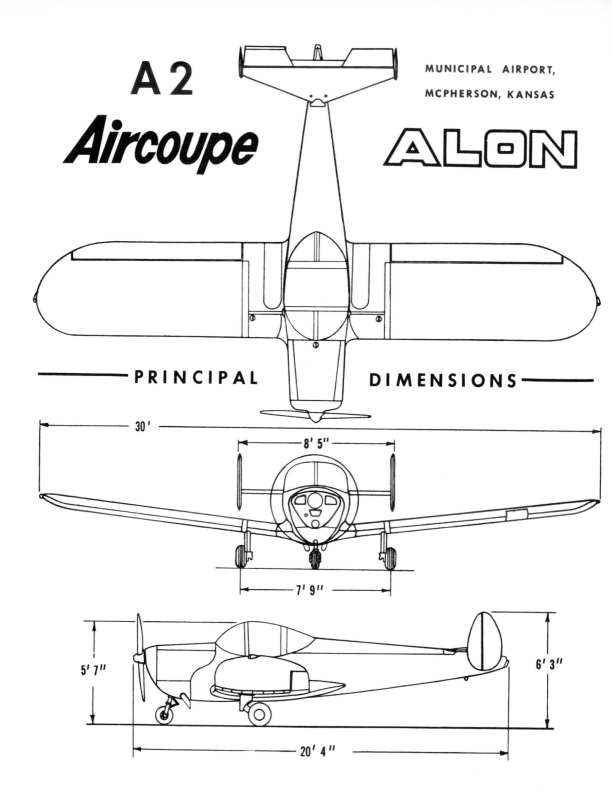

A 2
Aircoupe

MUNICIPAL AIRPORT,
MCPHERSON, KANSAS

ALON

PRINCIPAL — DIMENSIONS

30'

8' 5''

7' 9''

5' 7''

6' 3''

20' 4''

The original Ercoupe, produced by the Engineering Research Corporation (ERCO) of Riverdale, Maryland, in 1940, was designed by Fred Weick (who would later design the Piper Cherokee, among others) and was certified as nonspinnable. With limited control travel and no rudder pedals it was easy to fly and certainly one of the safest airplanes ever put into production. World War II stopped all pleasure flying, and the 65-hp Ercoupe 415-C was discontinued. It reappeared after the war as the 415-D powered with the 75-hp Continental C75-12. In 1948, the 415-E model was introduced with an 85-hp Continental. It was priced at $3,995, and you will pay that for a good one today.

No Ercoupes were built during the aircraft depression of the early fifties, but in 1956 Forney Aircraft Company of Fort Collins, Colorado, acquired Ercoupe manufacturing rights and began producing the Fornaire F-1 and F-2 Aircoupe. The Fornaire Aircoupes used the Continental C90-12 engine (the "-12" indicates starter and generator) and continued production through 1960. In 1963, Alon, Inc., of McPherson, Kansas, revived the design and offered the 90-hp Alon Aircoupe at $7,825.

Finally, Alon sold out to Mooney Aircraft Corporation in 1967, and Mooney so totally redesigned the little craft that it was not recognizable—or salable. (Mooney did some other stupid things about that time, which I will come to later.) However, ERCO, Forney, and Alon sold something over 6,000 Ercoupes/Aircoupes, and a good many are still flying. Seating is side-by-side, and the airframe is metal, with a metal-covered fuselage. The older ones have fabric-covered wings, and the later ones have rudder pedals.

Ercoupe/Aircoupe

	Ercoupe 415-G (85 hp)	Alon Aircoupe A2 (90 hp)
Wing span	30 ft	30 ft
Length	20 ft, 9 in	20 ft, 4 in
Height	5 ft, 11 in	5 ft, 7 in
Empty weight	838 lb	930 lb
Gross weight	1,400 lb	1,450 lb
Useful load	562 lb	520 lb
Wing loading	9.8 lb/sq ft	10.17 lb/sq ft
Power loading	16.47 lb/hp	16 lb/hp
Baggage capacity	75 lb	75 lb
Maximum speed	125 mph (109 kt)	129 mph (112 kt)
Cruising speed	110 mph (96 kt)	124 mph (108 kt)
Stalling speed	48 mph (42 kt)	52 mph (45 kt)
Initial climb	560 ft/min	600 ft/min
Service ceiling	11,000 ft	17,300 ft
Range (24 gal)	450 sm	444 sm

Mooney redesigned the Aircoupe and called it the Cadet. It met the fate it deserved in the marketplace.

Except for modern engines and materials, today's Great Lakes is little changed from the original classic design. Pictured is the modified 1932 Great Lakes flown by the late Hal Krier, three-time national aerobatic champion.

The original Great Lakes sport/trainer, 2T-1A, was built in Cleveland, Ohio, from 1929 through 1933 and was fitted with either the Cirrus or Menasco engine of 95–110 hp. The airplane was designed by Charles W. Meyers and Cliff Liesey. Meyers, who also designed the Waco Taperwing, was a World War I pilot, barnstormer, and test pilot who ended up as a senior captain for Eastern Airlines. Liesey, at last report, was still designing airplanes at Boeing.

The Great Lakes is a true classic. Its original engines—four-cylinder, in-line, air-cooled—were inadequate compromises because of the economic conditions of the time; but the Great Lakes was so easy to fly and land and had such amazing aerobatic potential that owners were soon installing the Warner radial engines of 125 and 145 hp, enlarging the vertical tail, and adding ailerons to the top wing.

After World War II most of the great U.S. akro pilots flew a Great Lakes so modified. One of the greatest, certainly the smoothest of them all, the late Harold Krier (three-time National Champion), performed his aerial ballet before millions during the fifties and sixties in a 1932 Great Lakes powered with a 185-hp Warner radial engine.

All this being so, no one should be surprised to learn that, when Doug Champlin of Enid, Oklahoma, began production of today's Great Lakes in 1973, he suffered no lack of customers, despite a price tag that crowded $20,000. It is closer to $30,000 now.

The Great Lakes Aircraft Company of Enid and Wichita (at this writing, the airframe is built in Wichita and the planes are finished in Enid, though rumor has it that the whole operation may soon be moved to larger facilities in McPherson, Kansas) offers two versions of the Great Lakes, the 2T-1A-1, powered with the Lycoming O-320-E2A of 140 hp, and the 2T-1A-2, fitted with the fuel-injected Lycoming IO-360-B1F6 of 180 hp. The 2T-1A-2 also has ailerons in the top wing, inverted fuel and oil systems, and a constant-speed prop. Both models are metal-framed and fabric-covered (would you believe grade-A cotton and butyrate dope?).

Great Lakes	Model 2T-1A-1	Model 2T-1A-2
Wing span	26 ft, 8 in	26 ft, 8 in
Length	20 ft, 2 in	20 ft, 2 in
Height	7 ft, 11 in	7 ft, 11 in
Empty weight	1,140 lb	1,230 lb
Gross weight	1,750 lb	1,800 lb
Useful load	610 lb	570 lb
Wing loading	9.33 lb/sq ft	9.63 lb/sq ft
Power loading	12.5 lb/hp	10 lb/hp
Baggage capacity	30 lb	40 lb
Maximum speed	120 mph (105 kt)	132 mph (115 kt)
Cruising speed	110 mph (95 kt)	118 mph (103 kt)
Stalling speed	48 mph (42 kt)	50 mph (44 kt)
Initial climb	1,000 ft/min	1,400 ft/min
Service ceiling	12,400 ft	17,000 ft
Range (26 gal)	300 sm	275 sm

41

Gulfstream-American Yankee/ Trainer, AA1, and TR2, Lynx, T-Cat

There is only one basic airframe involved with all these names and designations. It evolved from the BD-1, a Jim Bede design originally intended for the homebuilt airplane market in kit form. But Bede has always had a flair for designing sound airplanes with unsound price tags. So, American Aviation Corporation of Cleveland began building this neat little all-metal two-placer in 1968, calling it the Yankee. In 1971, the airplane received a new wing leading edge and optional "climb" propeller and was offered in two versions, the AA1 American Trainer and the TR2, the latter being a mite plusher and better equipped. Both versions were powered with the Lycoming O-235-C2C engine of 108 hp.

During the seventies, the two-place Gulfstream-Americans changed little except for some ever-wilder paint schemes, a switch (in the 1978 models) to the Lycoming O-235-L2C engine, which is rated at 115 hp and burns 100 octane fuel, and more exotic names. Thus, the TR2 had become the Lynx; and although a bare-bones AA1C Trainer was still available, it was somewhat more available as the T-Cat, an AA1C with extra equipment.

These airplanes are different. The structure is aluminum honeycomb, bonded—no rivets. They are small airplanes by any standard, though the cabins are roomy and comfortable. But mostly they are different to fly. Controls are sensitive, and there is little forgiveness in their nature. They are not for small fields; they come in fast and ignore all but the last couple of feet of ground cushion. They are slow climbers but very pleasant in cruise.

Gulfstream-American

	Trainer (108 hp)	Lynx (115 hp)
Wing span	24 ft, 6 in	24 ft, 6 in
Length	19 ft, 3 in	19 ft, 3 in
Height	7 ft, 6 in	7 ft, 6 in
Empty weight	980 lb	1,066 lb
Gross weight	1,560 lb	1,600 lb
Useful load	580 lb	534 lb
Wing loading	15 lb/sq ft	15.2 lb/sq ft
Power loading	14 lb/hp	13.9 lb/hp
Baggage capacity	100 lb	100 lb
Maximum speed	138 mph (120 kt)	140 mph (126 kt)
Cruising speed	124 mph (108 kt)	134 mph (117 kt)
Stalling speed	60 mph (53 kt)	60 mph (53 kt)
Initial climb	700 ft/min	700 ft/min
Service ceiling	12,750 ft	11,500 ft
Range (24 gal)	500 sm	525 sm

Luscombe Silvaire, 8A, 8E, and 8F

The Luscombe is another of those seemingly ageless airplanes that were so well conceived a generation or so ago that they are still sought after—and found—in the used market. The Silvaire 8F will easily equal any Cessna 150 in performance, and though the side-by-side seating is a little snug, the dual stick control is a tempting feature that tips off its unusual agility. It is necessary to pay attention when landing this airplane; its narrow landing gear has been known to allow a ground loop when carelessly handled on landing roll-out.

The first Silvaires were built in 1937, designed by Don Luscombe (also responsible for the famed Monocoupes), and were powered with engines ranging from 50 to 75 hp. After World War II the Silvaire was offered with 65 hp as the 8A model, with 85 hp as the 8E, and with 90 hp as the 8F until production stopped late in 1949.

During the early fifties, Texas Engineering and Manufacturing Company (TEMCO) took over the design and built a few Silvaires until, in 1955, Silvaire Aircraft Corporation was formed in Fort Collins, Colorado, to produce the 8F model. This company suspended production in 1960. So the Luscombe is not really an "old" airplane. After all, the Beechcraft Bonanza has been in continuous production since 1947, and the Cessna 180 since 1953. The really good designs give up little to time.

Luscombe Silvaire 8F

Wing span	35 ft	Baggage capacity	80 lb
Length	20 ft	Maximum speed	128 mph (112 kt)
Height	6 ft, 3 in	Cruising speed	120 mph (104 kt)
Empty weight	800 lb	Stalling speed	40 mph (35 kt)
Gross weight	1,300 lb	Initial climb	900 ft/min
Useful load	500 lb	Service ceiling	17,000 ft
Wing loading	9.2 lb/sq ft	Range (25 gal)	500 sm
Power loading	14.4 lb/hp		

The Luscombe Silvaire is an agile little craft with stick control and side-by-side seating.

43

Mooney Mite, Model 18

The single-place Mooney Mite is a delightful little craft that returns a lot of performance for only 65 hp. Only a few hundred were built, between 1950 and 1955 (the worst possible time to introduce a new airplane), but it managed to launch today's Mooney Aircraft Corporation. It is simple and easy to fly. Its retractable landing gear and its flaps are activated by muscle power through mechanical linkage, with no hydraulics or electric motors to service or maintain. The Mite's only drawback, as I see it, is its wooden construction and plywood covering.

Mooney Mite, Model 18

Wing span	26 ft, 10 in	Baggage capacity	75 lb
Length	17 ft, 7 in	Maximum speed	138 mph (130 kt)
Height	6 ft, 2 in	Cruising speed	125 mph (109 kt)
Empty weight	500 lb	Stalling speed	40 mph (35 kt)
Gross weight	850 lb	Initial climb	1,000 ft/min
Useful load	350 lb	Service ceiling	19,400 ft
Wing loading	8.9 lb/sq ft	Range (16 gal)	500 sm
Power loading	13.1 lb/hp		

The first Piper airplane—the 40-hp J-3 Cub—evolved from the E-2 and J-2 Taylor Cubs, and was introduced in 1938. By 1940, the J-3 had received the Continental A65 engine, and the yellow Cubs were the most popular civilian training planes in America. They were gentle machines that cruised at a leisurely 65 mph and required a bare minimum of a landing patch. They would forgive a student pilot almost anything and were fun to fly—fun, perhaps, because they demanded so little from their pilots.

A lot of Cubs were built—about 2,000 prior to World War II, and nearly 6,000 more during the war as Army L-4's—and production extended into 1947, when the J-3 was finally displaced by the Cub Special, PA-11. The Special employed the J-3 airframe but had an 18-gal wing tank and full-cowled engine. It was offered with both the 65-hp engine and the Continental C90. The PA-11 production halted in 1949, when the first Super Cub PA-18 was announced. It was available with either the 90-hp Continental or the 108-hp Lycoming O-235. The Super Cub has remained in production ever since. Many were built with 125 hp, but only the 150-hp model was available in the late seventies, fitted with the Lycoming O-320.

The modern PA-18 still looks very much like a J-3, but you can guess what all that additional power has done for it. The Super Cub with 125 hp or more is a true utility aircraft, but a good load carrier, a working airplane. And it is still fun to fly.

Piper Cub J-3, and Super Cub PA-18

The Piper J-3 Cub makes few demands on its pilot and is as much fun to fly today as when it first appeared in 1938.

45

Piper Cub J-3 and Piper Super Cub PA-18-150

	J-3 model (65 hp)	PA-18 model (150 hp)
Wing span	35 ft, 2 in	35 ft, 4 in
Length	22 ft, 5 in	22 ft, 6 in
Height	6 ft, 8 in	6 ft, 8 in
Empty weight	680 lb	930 lb
Gross weight	1,160 lb	1,750 lb
Useful load	480 lbs	820 lb
Wing loading	6.18 lb/sq ft	10 lb/sq ft
Power loading	22 lb/hp	11.6 lb/hp
Maximum speed	87 mph (72 kt)	130 mph (113 kt)
Cruising speed	70 mph (62 kt)	115 mph (100 kt)
Stalling speed	38 mph (34 kt)	43 mph (38 kt)
Initial climb	450 ft/min	960 ft/min
Service ceiling	12,000 ft	19,000 ft
Range	200 sm (12 gal)	460 sm (36 gal)

Piper Cruiser J-5 and Super Cruiser J-5C (PA-12)

Production of the 75-hp three-place (barely) J-5 Piper Cruiser began early in 1941, was interrupted by World War II, and resumed in 1946 as the Super Cruiser with a choice of engines, 100 or 108 hp. Fitted with the 108-hp Lycoming, this craft became the PA-12, the most popular version. Seating is tandem, with a single pilot's seat in front and a bench seat in the rear that accommodates two.

The Super Cruiser's airframe is typical Piper for that era, metal-framed and fabric-covered, with the appearance of a fattened Cub and flight characteristics to match.

Piper Super Cruiser, Model PA-12

Wing span	35 ft, 5 in	Baggage capacity	40 lb
Length	22 ft, 6 in	Maximum speed	114 mph (100 kt)
Height	6 ft, 10 in	Cruising speed	100 mph (87 kt)
Empty weight	855 lb	Stalling speed	42 mph (37 kt)
Gross weight	1,550 lb	Initial climb	650 ft/min
Useful load	695 lb	Service ceiling	12,000 ft
Wing loading	8.6 lb/sq ft	Range (25 gal)	420 sm
Power loading	15.5 lb/hp		

Piper Vagabond, Models PA-15 and PA-17

The two Vagabond models appeared in 1948, the PA-15 being the stripped version, without even a floor mat or cabin heater, to allow a selling price of $1,995. Seating was side by side, and the engine was the 65-hp Lycoming O-145. A lot of people have questioned the 65-hp rating of this engine, because it has a piston displacement of 144.5 cu in., whereas the 65-hp Continental engine has a displacement of 171 cu in. And pilots who have flown J-3 Cubs

The Piper PA-18 Super Cub has been in production since 1949, fitted with engines ranging in power from 90 hp to 150 hp.

The Piper PA-12 Super Cruiser seats three and is powered with the O-235 Lycoming engine of 108 hp. The 100-hp version of this craft was the J-5C model.

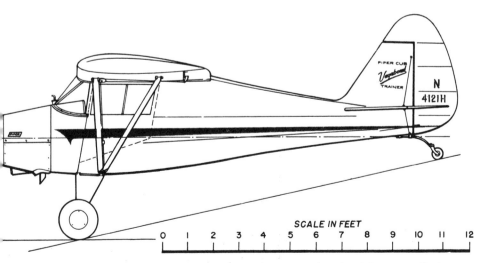

SCALE IN FEET

0 1 2 3 4 5 6 7 8 9 10 11 12

The Piper Vagabond is no longer plentiful in the used market, but it is an excellent minimum-cost fun machine.

powered with both will tell you that the Continental-powered Cub has significantly more muscle. There is an old saying among enginemen that "there's no substitute for cubic inches." This is probably why Piper introduced the PA-17 Vagabond only a month or so after the PA-15 was announced. The PA-17 was fitted with the Continental A65, and it had shock absorbers, floor mats, and other extras the PA-15 lacked.

The PA-17 is hard to beat for a minimum-cost personal/fun airplane. Like all first-generation Pipers, it is easy to fly and cheap to maintain. It is more compact than a Cub and will cruise at 90 mph true on 4 gals/h.

Piper Colt PA-22-108

About 2,000 Piper Colts were built in 1960–62, but the company directed most of its energy to the introduction and expansion of the new Cherokee series. The Colts were simply two-place versions of the popular four-place Tri-Pacers that had been on the market since 1951. Fitted with Lycoming O-235 engines of 108 hp, the Colts were honest, if unremarkable, machines. Most, perhaps, are still flying and returning a goodly portion of pleasure per dollar spent. The Colt, like all two-place Pipers prior to the Cherokees, had wooden spars, but is otherwise metal-framed and fabric-covered. (One exception: some late model J-3 Cubs have metal spars.)

Piper Vagabond PA-17 and Colt PA-22-108

	Vagabond PA-17	Colt PA-22-108
Wing span	29 ft, 3 in	30 ft
Length	18 ft, 7 in	20 ft
Height	6 ft	6 ft, 3 in
Empty weight	620 lb	940 lb
Gross weight	1,100 lb	1,650 lb
Useful load	480 lb	710 lb
Wing loading	7.5 lb/sq ft	11.2 lb/sq ft
Power loading	16.8 lb/hp	15.3 lb/hp
Baggage capacity	40 lb	100 lb
Maximum speed	100 mph (87 kt)	120 mph (104 kt)
Cruising speed	90 mph (78 kt)	115 mph (100 kt)
Stalling speed	45 mph (39 kt)	54 mph (47 kt)
Initial climb	510 ft/min	610 ft/min
Service ceiling	10,000 ft	12,000 ft
Range	250 sm (12 gal)	345 sm (18 gal)

The Piper Colts were built from 1960 to 1962 as 108-hp, two-place versions of the popular Tri-Pacer.

The Cruiser is the deluxe version of the smallest Cherokee; it may be fitted with rear seats.

The first two-place Cherokee was the 140B, introduced in 1963, two years after the original 150-hp four-place Cherokee appeared. Actually, Piper regards all the 150-hp Cherokees as "optional four-place" airplanes, but with full tanks these craft have but 600 lb remaining for people and baggage.

The all-metal Cherokee is generally regarded as the easiest to fly of all trainers in production today; some instructors feel that it is too easy, too forgiving, and therefore does not sharpen students' skills to a sufficient degree. But people used to say the same thing about the J-3 Cub, and a lot of senior airline captains today learned to fly in a J-3.

In 1972, the Cherokees were given a new rudder and dorsal fin, and Piper dropped the 140 designation and renamed the 150-hp trainers the Cruiser and Flite Liner, the Cruiser being the deluxe model with the extras, including wheel pants and an instrument flight rules (IFR) panel.

Except for a slight increase in empty weight, the specifications and performance figures for the 140, Cruiser, and Flite Liner have not changed over the years. The seventy or so additional pounds have been invested in such things as better soundproofing, cabin climate control, dual toe brakes, and improved nose-wheel steering.

Piper Cherokee 140B, Flite Liner, and Cruiser, Model PA-28

Piper Cherokee Cruiser

Wing span	30 ft	Baggage capacity	200 lb
Length	23 ft, 4 in	Maximum speed	142 mph (123 kt)
Height	7 ft, 4 in	Cruising speed	135 mph (117 kt)
Empty weight	1,274 lb	Stalling speed	55 mph (48 kt)
Gross weight	2,150 lb	Initial climb	630 ft/min
Useful load	876 lb	Service ceiling	10,950 ft
Wing loading	13.4 lb/sq ft	Range (34 gal)	510 sm
Power loading	14.3 lb/hp		

Akro champion Gene Soucey and the Pitts S-1 Special.

Pitts Special S-1S and S-2A

The two-place Pitts aerobatic biplane grew from the famed Pitts Specials, the tiny, single-place machines that were gradually refined over a twenty-five-year period, from the original 55-hp sport airplanes to the 180- and 200-hp world championship aerobatic planes of today. Plans for the two-aileron S-1 Special were made available to amateur plane builders in 1962; the modern Pitts, with symmetrical airfoils and four ailerons, appeared in 1966. The two-place version, the S-2, was introduced that same year. But not until 1973 were these airplanes at last certified by the FAA and put into production.

Pitts construction is conventional: 4130 steel tube fuselage, all-wood wings, and Ceconite covering. The guaranteed load factors are 9 positive Gs and 4.5 negative Gs.

Everyone agrees that Stits controls are highly sensitive, with instant response in all axes—that roll-rate is fantastic; that there is no forward vision on the ground or in landing attitude; and that these machines, while a ball to fly, demand precise technique (or a certain amount of good luck) to land without visible disaster. In short, the Pitts models are not toys; they have to be *flown* from the time you check the oil until you close the hangar door on them.

Several hundred of the Pitts have been constructed by amateur builders, and these will be licensed in the Experimental category. The homebuilts will show up in the used market alongside the factory-produced Pitts, which possess Approved Type Certificates. A homebuilt Pitts may be as well crafted as one that comes from Curtis Pitts' factory—but the odds are against it. Before buying a homebuilt anything, you really should check with the FAA inspector who okayed the work on it. You will find him at the regional GADO (General Aviation District office). Most of the homebuilt Pitts will have a gentler airfoil, two ailerons, and 125–150 hp. The factory-built S-1S Special will be powered with the Lycoming IO-360-B4A engine of 180 hp with a fixed-pitch prop. The two-place S-2A (for which plans have not been released to the homebuilders) is fitted with the Lycoming IO-360-A1A, rated at 200 hp, and equipped with a constant-speed propeller.

Pitts Special S-1S and S-2A

	S-1S (single-place)	S-2A (two-place)
Wing span	17 ft, 4 in	20 ft
Length	14 ft, 3 in	17 ft, 9 in
Height	6 ft	6 ft, 4.5 in
Empty weight	720 lb	1,000 lb
Gross weight	1,150 lb	1,500 lb
Useful load	420 lb	500 lb
Wing loading	11.4 lb/sq ft	11.2 lb/sq ft
Power loading	6.38 lb/hp	7.5 lb/hp
Baggage capacity	None	20 lb
Maximum speed	147 mph (128 kt)	157 mph (137 kt)
Cruising speed	143 mph (124 kt)	152 mph (132 kt)
Stalling speed	64 mph (56 kt)	58 mph (51 kt)
Initial climb	2,600 ft/min	1,900 ft/min
Fuel capacity	20 gal	24 gal

Taylorcraft BC-12D and F-19

The first Taylorcraft was the 40-hp B12 model of 1937, produced by E. Gilbert Taylor in Alliance, Ohio, following Taylor's split with William Piper. The "T-Craft" had 65 hp by 1941, and when production was resumed after the war with the BC-12D model, nearly 3,000 were built before the company folded in 1947.

The BC-12Ds will outperform the J-3 Cub with the same horsepower, apparently because of a more efficient wing. Seating is side by side and the airframe is all metal (except for a spruce wing spar) and fabric-covered.

In 1974, a new company in Alliance announced production of the F-19 Taylorcraft Sportsman, a reengineered version of the BC-12D fitted with the Continental 0-200 engine of 100 hp. This company has been moderately successful to date.

Taylorcraft BC-12D and F-19

The BC-12D "T-Craft" outperforms the J-3 Cub using the same engine. A modern version, with 100 hp, is the F-19 Sportsman, built in Alliance, Ohio.

	BC-12D (65 hp)	F-19 (100 hp)
Wing span	36 ft	36 ft
Length	22 ft	22 ft, 1 in
Height	6 ft, 6 in	6 ft, 6 in
Empty weight	750 lb	870 lb
Gross weight	1,200 lb	1,500 lb
Useful load	450 lb	630 lb
Wing loading	6.5 lb/sq ft	8.2 lb/sq ft
Power loading	18.5 lb/hp	15 lb/hp
Baggage capacity	None	72 lb
Maximum speed	100 mph (87 kt)	127 mph (111 kt)
Cruising speed	95 mph (85 kt)	115 mph (100 kt)
Stalling speed	38 mph (33 kt)	43 mph (38 kt)
Initial climb	900 ft/min	775 ft/min
Service ceiling	15,000 ft	18,000 ft
Range	300 sm (12 gal)	400 sm (24 gal)

The Globe/Temco Swift is another outstanding design produced during the late 1940s and still popular, offering good low-cost cross-country ability.

Temco (Globe) Swift, Model GC-1B

The Temco Swift was built between 1946 and 1950 by Texas Engineering and Manufacturing Company of Dallas, which took over the design from Globe Aircraft Corporation of neighboring Fort Worth. The Temco Swifts, offered with both 125- and 145-hp engines, are excellent all-metal craft with side-by-side seating and a retractable landing gear. Control surfaces are fabric-covered. There are still some Globe-built Swifts around, but most are Temcos.

The metal Swifts have undeservedly suffered from a poor reputation earned by the original plywood-covered Globe Swift, which had an 85-hp engine and undesirable spin characteristics. The higher-horsepower metal machines are different airplanes and possess no undesirable traits. These craft sold new for $4,995, but you can easily pay twice that for a really good one today.

Temco Swift GC-1B (125 hp)

Wing span	29 ft, 4 in	Baggage capacity	40 lb
Length	20 ft, 10 in	Maximum speed	150 mph (131 kt)
Height	6 ft, 1 in	Cruising speed	140 mph (122 kt)
Empty weight	1,118 lb	Stalling speed	48 mph (42 kt)
Gross weight	1,710 lb	Initial climb	1,000 ft/min
Useful load	525 lb	Service ceiling	16,000 ft
Wing loading	13 lb/sq ft	Range (26 gal)	425 sm
Power loading	13.7 lb/hp		

The Varga Kachina is a gentle sport plane with a military accent.

The Varga Kachina may resemble a malnourished BT-13 as some of the aging World War II tigers claim, but that is not necessarily a put-down. The BT-13 Vibrator (actually, Valiant) is much revered by most gray eagles who trained in them, and I am not altogether sure that the Kachina's designer, World War II pilot Bill Morrisey, did not consciously pay his respects to that famous Vultee when he drew up plans, back in 1950, for the Morrisey 2150 sport/trainer. (*Kachina* is a Hopi Indian god, I am informed by Keith Connes, editor of *Air Progress* Magazine.)

Morrisey's little company produced a handful of these craft before selling out to the Shinn company, which in turn built perhaps as many as 50 Shinn 2150s during the early sixties. Then, in 1974, George Varga, an aircraft parts supplier, negotiated for the manufacturing rights and began production a year later of the Varga Kachina at a plant in Chandler, Arizona.

The Kachina is powered with the Lycoming O-320-A of 150 hp, is all-metal, and has tandem seating. This plane flies nicely, and though it has not been certified for aerobatics at this writing, it probably will be when the 180-hp version appears.

Varga Kachina (Morrisey/ Shinn Model 2150)

Varga Kachina

Wing span	30 ft	Baggage capacity	50 lb
Length	21 ft	Maximum speed	148 mph (129 kt)
Height	7 ft	Cruising speed	135 mph (117 kt)
Empty weight	1,125 lb	Stalling speed	52 mph (45 kt)
Gross weight	1,817 lb	Initial climb	1,450 ft/min
Useful load	692 lb	Service ceiling	22,000 ft
Wing loading	12.05 lb/sq ft	Range (35 gal)	525 sm
Power loading	12.12 lb/hp		

4

Used Four/Six-Place Airplanes, Fixed Landing Gear

The four- to six-place airplanes with fixed landing gear represent the largest single segment of the general aviation fleet. These are clearly the most practical machines for most people. Cessna has dominated this market since the mid-fifties, with the Piper Cherokee muscling in for a sizable piece of the action since the mid-sixties.

Both Cessna and Piper have been successful at this level because they produce airplanes that may be safely operated in comfort by any reasonably normal person. The superman era of flight passed with an earlier generation, and today's lightplane buyer is more interested in the convenience of flying than in any macho image it may impart. He or she will therefore gladly trade some speed, range, and useful load for comfort and ease of operation. Fun is fun, and business is business, and there is no point in unnecessarily complicating either one.

Most of the four-placers with fixed landing gear are in the medium horsepower—125–180 hp—range and most will have fixed-pitch propellers.

Aero Commander, Model 100, Darter, and Lark

The Aero Commander 100 Darter was formerly the Volaire. Production life was short.

The Aero Commander 100 was originally produced as the Volaire in Aliquippa, Pennsylvania, but few were built before the design was acquired by Aero Commander (now a division of Rockwell International) in 1966.

Powered with the Lycoming O-320-A of 150 hp, the AC-100 has a steel tube fuselage frame through the cabin area and a semimonocoque aft fuselage. It is all-metal, with an internal fiberglass slab shock absorber for the main gear. Brakes are operated by a single hand lever similar to that of the Tri-Pacer. It has good flight characteristics, though it is not as docile as a Skyhawk or Cherokee.

In 1968, Aero Commander announced the Darter Commander, which was the AC-100 with a new paint job, and the Lark Commander, which was the same airplane with a swept rudder and 180 hp. But none of these airplanes sold well and production soon halted.

The Aero Commander Lark is a 180-hp version of the AC-100 Darter. Relatively few were built during 1968.

Aero Commander Model 100

Wing span	35 ft	Baggage capacity	120 lb
Length	22 ft, 6 in	Maximum speed	142 mph (123 kt)
Height	9 ft, 4 in	Cruising speed	128 mph (112 kt)
Empty weight	1,275 lb	Stalling speed	48 mph (42 kt)
Gross weight	2,250 lb	Initial climb	850 ft/min
Useful load	975 lb	Service ceiling	13,000 ft
Wing loading	12.2 lb/sq ft	Range	650 sm
Power loading	14.7 lb/hp		

Beechcraft Musketeer, Model 23, Custom, Super, and Sundowner

Beech's fixed-gear four-seaters began with the Model 23 Musketeer in 1962. This airplane was powered with the Lycoming O-320-02B of 160 hp and introduced honeycomb bonded construction (in its laminar flow wings) to the lightplane field. The Musketeers have been refined over the years as the line expanded, and in 1972 the name *Musketeer* was dropped, leaving the 150-hp Model 19 Sport, the 180-hp Model 23 Sundowner, and the 200-hp retractable-gear Model 24 Sierra.

However, between 1962 and 1972 there were some other Musketeers. The first Musketeer was in production until June 1964, when the Musketeer II appeared with a fuel-injected Continental of 165 hp and an extra window on each side. The "Three Musketeers" were announced for 1966, when Beech reverted to 150 hp for the Sport III; the 165-hp model became the Custom III, and a new Super III was added with 200 hp.

55

In 1968, the Custom III went to 180 hp and was also offered in an aerobatic version. This made a total of five Musketeers because the 150-hp Sport was also offered in an aerobatic version.

In 1970, the Musketeer fuselage was redesigned, with the addition of 4.5 in. across the front seats and reshaped windows. The Super model was offered with an optional fourth window on each side, along with an additional bench seat aft to make it a six-place airplane.

Since the name *Musketeer* was dropped, the fixed-gear Beechcrafts have been the B19 Sport and the C23 Sundowner. These aircraft changed little during the middle and late seventies except for new paint jobs and higher prices. The first Model 23 was priced at $13,300 in January 1962. The 1978 C23 was priced at $31,750.

Beechcraft Musketeer II, Custom III, Super 200, and Sundowner

The first Beechcraft Model 23 Musketeer was introduced in 1962, powered with the Lycoming O-320 engine of 160 hp.

Construction details of the Beechcraft Model 23 wing.

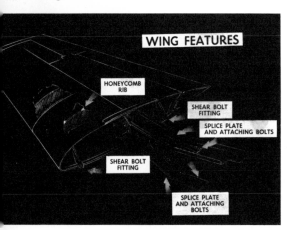

WING FEATURES

HONEYCOMB RIB

SHEAR BOLT FITTING

SPLICE PLATE AND ATTACHING BOLTS

SHEAR BOLT FITTING

SPLICE PLATE AND ATTACHING BOLTS

	Musketeer II	Custom III
Wing span	32 ft, 9 in	32 ft, 9 in
Length	25 ft	25 ft
Height	8 ft, 3 in	8 ft, 3 in
Empty weight	1,398 lb	1,375 lb
Gross weight	2,350 lb	2,450 lb
Useful load	952 lb	1,085 lb
Wing loading	15.87 lb/sq ft	16.78 lb/sq ft
Power loading	14.12 lb/hp	13.61 lb/hp
Baggage capacity	140 lb	140 lb
Maximum speed	146 mph (127 kt)	145 mph (126 kt)
Cruising speed	137 mph (118 kt)	143 mph (124 kt)
Stalling speed	62 mph (54 kt)	59 mph (52 kt)
Initial climb	770 ft/min	820 ft/min
Service ceiling	12,550 ft	13,650 ft
Range (40 gal)	570 sm	420 sm

	Super 200	Sundowner
Wing span	32 ft, 9 in	32 ft, 9 in
Length	25 ft	25 ft, 9 in
Height	8 ft, 3 in	8 ft, 3 in
Empty weight	1,410 lb	1,425 lb
Gross weight	2,550 lb	2,450 lb
Useful load	1,140 lb	1,025 lb
Wing loading	17.47 lb/sq ft	16.08 lb/sq ft
Power loading	12.75 lb/hp	12.25 lb/hp
Baggage capacity	270 lb	270 lb
Maximum speed	158 mph (137 kt)	151 mph (131 kt)
Cruising speed	150 mph (130 kt)	143 mph (125 kt)
Stalling speed	61 mph (53 kt)	60 mph (52 kt)
Initial climb	880 ft/min	820 ft/min
Service ceiling	14,850 ft	13,650 ft
Range	385 sm (40 gal)*	685 sm (60 gal)

*60 gal optional

The Beechcraft Musketeer Custom, with 180 hp, seats four to six.

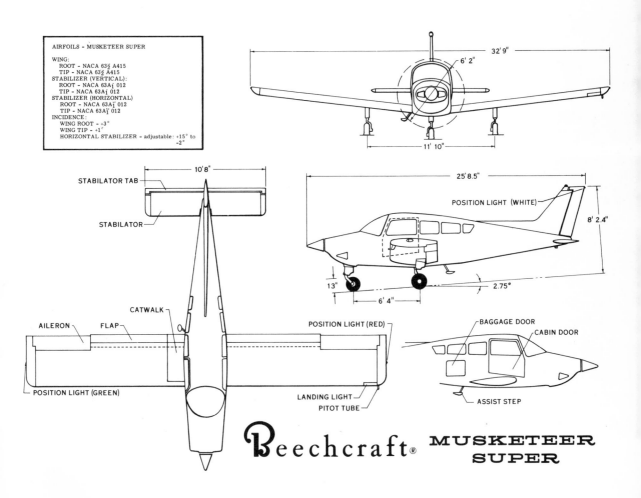

AIRFOILS - MUSKETEER SUPER

WING:
    ROOT - NACA 63½ A415
    TIP - NACA 63½ A415
STABILIZER (VERTICAL):
    ROOT - NACA 63A₁' 012
    TIP - NACA 63A₁' 012
STABILIZER (HORIZONTAL)
    ROOT - NACA 63A₁' 012
    TIP - NACA 63A₁' 012
INCIDENCE:
    WING ROOT - +3°
    WING TIP - +1°
    HORIZONTAL STABILIZER - adjustable: +15° to -2°

32' 9"
6' 2"
11' 10"

10' 8"
STABILATOR TAB
STABILATOR

25' 8.5"
POSITION LIGHT (WHITE)
8' 2.4"
13"
6' 4"
2.75°

AILERON FLAP   CATWALK
POSITION LIGHT (GREEN)
POSITION LIGHT (RED)
LANDING LIGHT
PITOT TUBE

BAGGAGE DOOR
CABIN DOOR
ASSIST STEP

Beechcraft® MUSKETEER SUPER

Beechcraft Model
C23 Sundowner.

ℬeechcraft SUNDOWNER 180 MODEL C23

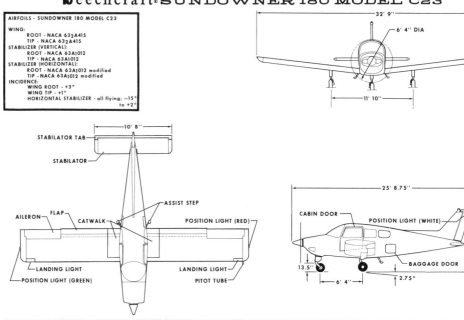

AIRFOILS - SUNDOWNER 180 MODEL C23

WING:
ROOT - NACA 63₂A415
TIP - NACA 63₂A415
STABILIZER (VERTICAL):
ROOT - NACA 63A1012
TIP - NACA 63A1012
STABILIZER (HORIZONTAL):
ROOT - NACA 63A1012 modified
TIP - NACA 63A1012 modified
INCIDENCE:
WING ROOT - +3°
WING TIP - +1°
HORIZONTAL STABILIZER - all flying; —15°
to +2°

The 1977 Skyhawk II/100 (top)
and Hawk XP.

58

The Cessna 170 was built 1948–57. The first ones had fabric-covered wings and two lift struts on each side. The 1949 Model 170A had a metal-covered wing, a single lift strut on each side, and a dorsal fin. The 170B, which appeared in 1952, added L-19-type flaps. The 170 and 170A were equipped with the Continental C-145-2 engine of 145 hp; the 170Bs were fitted with either a C-145-2 or the O-300-A, the latter also rated at 145 hp.

The 170s are easy to fly and compare well in performance with the 172s and Skyhawks that followed them. These are stable airplanes, stalls are gentle, and recommended cruise setting of these engines is 2,500 rpm, which results in 120 mph true on 8 gal/h. The 170s have no special maintenance problem and are much sought after in the used market.

Cessna 170, 170A, and 170B

Cessna 170A and 1957 Model Cessna 172

	170A (1951)	172 (1957)
Wing span	36 ft	36 ft
Length	25 ft	25 ft
Height	6 ft, 7 in	8 ft, 6 in
Empty weight	1,185 lb	1,260 lb
Gross weight	2,200 lb	2,200 lb
Useful load	985 lb	940 lb
Wing loading	12.8 lb/sq ft	12.6 lb/sq ft
Power loading	15.5 lb/hp	15.5 lb/hp
Baggage capacity	75 lb	120 lb
Maximum speed	135 mph (117 kt)	135 mph (117 kt)
Cruising speed	120 mph (104 kt)	124 mph (108 kt)
Stalling speed	53 mph (47 kt)	55 mph (49 kt)
Initial climb	650 ft/min	660 ft/min
Service ceiling	15,500 ft	13,300 ft
Range	640 sm (36 gal)	620 sm (42 gal)

The Cessna 172 for 1964.

The Cessna 172/Skyhawk (the Skyhawk is the deluxe version and far and away the most popular) has been built in such numbers—something over 30,000 at this writing—that it almost seems pointless to describe this series. The 172/Skyhawk engine was the Continental O-300 of 145 hp until 1968, when a switch was made to the Lycoming O-320-EZD of 150 hp. The Lycoming has a time between overhaul (TBO) of 2,000 h, whereas the recommended TBO for the O-300 is 1,200 h.

Some major improvements, and a host of minor ones, have accrued to these craft since the Skyhawk version appeared in 1961. The swept rudder and big rear window were added in 1964; conical wingtips were offered in 1970; tubular steel gear legs in 1971; a modified airfoil for improved slow-flight characteristics in 1973; the Clark Y propeller airfoil the following year; and a quieter cabin with slightly reshaped rudder in 1976. The 1977 Skyhawk/100 brought another engine change, the Lycoming O-320-H2AD of 160 hp, which is rated for 100-octane fuel. This adds slightly to performance while apparently burning no more fuel than the previous engines. The 1978

Cessna 172 and Skyhawk

Skyhawk gained a 28-v electrical system to better handle the increasing avionics loads, and an optional air conditioner.

The Skyhawk II version, introduced in 1974, is a standard Skyhawk with dual controls, a factory-installed nav/comm package, beacons, and ELT.

The Hawk XP version appeared in 1977 fitted with the Continental IO-360-K engine of 195 hp and constant-speed propeller. It is also offered as the Hawk XP II with the extra goodies.

Cessna 172/Skyhawk (150 hp, 1975) and Skyhawk 100 (160 hp, 1977)

	172/Skyhawk	Skyhawk 100
Wing span	35 ft, 10 in	35 ft, 10 in
Length	26 ft, 11 in	26 ft, 11 in
Height	8 ft, 9.5 in	8 ft, 9.5 in
Empty weight	1,350 lb	1,379 lb
Gross weight	2,300 lb	2,300 lb
Useful load	950 lb	921 lb
Wing loading	13.2 lb/sq ft	13.2 lb/sq ft
Power loading	15.3 lb/hp	14.4 lb/hp
Baggage capacity	120 lb	120 lb
Maximum speed	144 mph (125 kt)	144 mph (125 kt)
Cruising speed	138 mph (119 kt)	140 mph (122 kt)
Stalling speed	49 mph (43 kt)	50 mph (44 kt)
Initial climb	645 ft/min	770 ft/min
Service ceiling	13,100 ft	14,200 ft
Range	650 sm (42 gal)	485 sm (43 gal)

Interior of the 1977 Skyhawk II/100.

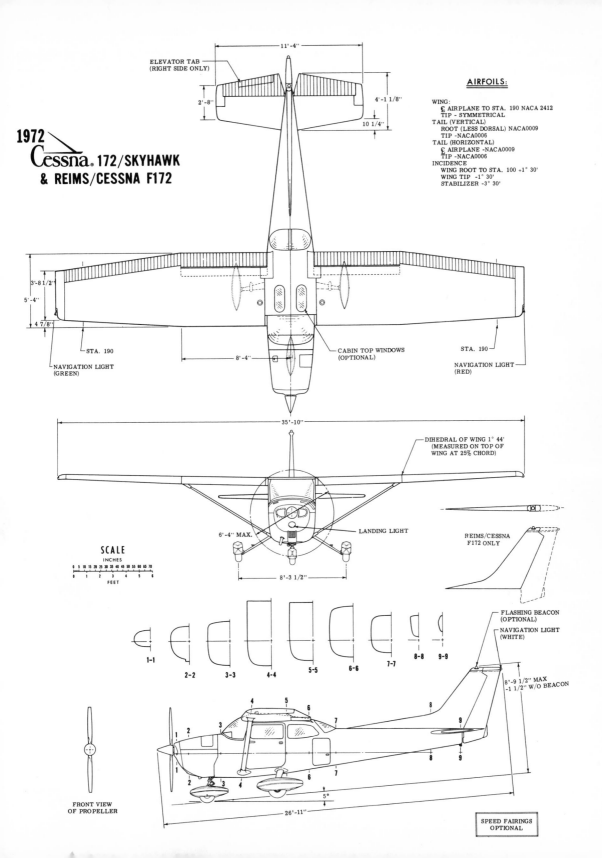

1972
Cessna. 172/SKYHAWK
& REIMS/CESSNA F172

ELEVATOR TAB
(RIGHT SIDE ONLY)

11'-4"
4'-1 1/8"
2'-8"
10 1/4"

AIRFOILS:

WING:
℄ AIRPLANE TO STA. 190 NACA 2412
TIP - SYMMETRICAL
TAIL (VERTICAL)
ROOT (LESS DORSAL) NACA0009
TIP -NACA0006
TAIL (HORIZONTAL)
℄ AIRPLANE -NACA0009
TIP -NACA0006
INCIDENCE
WING ROOT TO STA. 100 +1° 30'
WING TIP -1° 30'
STABILIZER -3° 30'

3'-8 1/2"
5'-4"
4 7/8"

STA. 190

NAVIGATION LIGHT
(GREEN)

CABIN TOP WINDOWS
(OPTIONAL)

8'-4"

STA. 190

NAVIGATION LIGHT
(RED)

35'-10"

DIHEDRAL OF WING 1° 44'
(MEASURED ON TOP OF
WING AT 25% CHORD)

6'-4" MAX.

LANDING LIGHT

8'-3 1/2"

REIMS/CESSNA
F172 ONLY

FLASHING BEACON
(OPTIONAL)

NAVIGATION LIGHT
(WHITE)

8'-9 1/2" MAX
-1 1/2" W/O BEACON

SCALE
INCHES
0 5 10 15 20 25 30 35 40 45 50 55 60 65 70
0 1 2 3 4 5 6
FEET

1-1
2-2
3-3
4-4
5-5
6-6
7-7
8-8
9-9

5°

FRONT VIEW
OF PROPELLER

26'-11"

SPEED FAIRINGS
OPTIONAL

Cessna Model 175/Powermatic (Skylark)

The Cessna 175 Skylark was brought out in 1958 and produced into 1963—by which time Cessna was calling it the 172 Powermatic. This airplane has the standard 172/Skyhawk airframe of that period but is powered with the Continental GO-300-E engine, rated at 175 hp, along with a constant-speed propeller. The GO-300-E is a geared engine that produces its rated power at 3,200 crankshaft rpm while the propeller is turning 2,400 rpm. Since the propeller reduction-gear box is located above the driveshaft on the front of the engine, the same 84-in. prop as used on the 145-hp versions gains several inches ground clearance on the Skylark/Powermatics. These craft sold new for about $3,000 more than contemporary Skyhawks. The 1963 Skyhawk was priced at $11,995 f.a.f.

Cessna Hawk XP (195 hp, 1977) and Model 175/Powermatic (175 hp, 1963)

	Hawk XP	Powermatic
Wing span	35 ft, 10 in	36 ft, 2 in
Length	27 ft, 2 in	26 ft, 6 in
Height	8 ft, 9.5 in	8 ft, 11 in
Empty weight	1,549 lb	1,360 lb
Gross weight	2,550 lb	2,500 lb
Useful load	1,001 lb	950 lb
Wing loading	14.7 lb/sq ft	14.4 lb/sq ft
Power loading	13.1 lb/hp	14.3 lb/hp
Baggage capacity	200 lb	120 lb
Maximum speed	154 mph (134 kt)	146 mph (127 kt)
Cruising speed	151 mph (131 kt)	138 mph (119 kt)
Stalling speed	62 mph (53 kt)	55 mph (48 kt)
Initial climb	870 ft/min	830 ft/min
Service ceiling	17,000 ft	17,000 ft
Range (52 gal)	557 sm	540 sm

Cessna 180 and 185 Skywagons

The Cessna 180 has been in continuous production since 1953, longer than any other Cessna. Approximately 9,000 have been built to date. This airplane was designed as a ranch and bush craft, with outstanding short-field performance and good load-carrying ability. It is all of that, and something more, because a lot of them are not working for their keep in the boonies but are flown for pleasure and business. The 180 is too pleasant, too practical, too versatile to be typecast.

The 180 has not changed much over the years. It went from a 225-hp Continental to the Continental O-470 of 230 hp in 1956; it gained an extra window on each side in 1970, along with bigger fuel tanks and reshaped gear legs. Its empty weight went from 1,500 in 1953 to 1,600 in 1978, and its gross weight went from 2,550 lb in 1953 to 2,800 lb in 1978. Of course, all airplanes gain weight with age, mostly because people insist on more comfort.

The 180's cabin is simple, as befits a working airplane, but it will easily accommodate six big people without cutting down on your fuel supply.

The 1978 Cessna 180 Skywagon was basically unchanged from the first Cessna 180 built in 1953.

The Cessna 185 Skywagon is like the 180, except 500 pounds more so.

The Cessna 185 is a 180 with more power. The 185 really is a Skywagon. Cessna says it is built a mite stronger here and there, although the only noticeable difference in appearance between it and the 180 is a large dorsal fin. The 185 was introduced in 1961 and was powered with the Continental IO-470-F of 260 hp through the 185E model of 1966. But also that year the 185 was offered with the Continental IO-520-D of 300 hp, and in 1967 the 260-hp version was discontinued. A lot of detail improvements have accrued since then, although the 185 has remained essentially the same airplane. We can sum it up by saying that the 185 has approximately the same performance as the 180 while carrying 500 lb more useful load.

Cessna 180 and 185 Skywagons

	Model 180 (1970)	Model 185 (1978)
Wing span	35 ft, 10 in	35 ft, 10 in
Length	25 ft, 9 in	25 ft, 9 in
Height	7 ft, 9 in	7 ft, 9 in
Empty weight	1,560 lb	1,690 lb
Gross weight	2,800 lb	3,350 lb
Useful load	1,240 lb	1,672 lb
Wing loading	16.1 lb/sq ft	19.3 lb/sq ft
Power loading	12.2 lb/hp	11.3 lb/hp
Baggage capacity	400 lb	170 lb normal
Maximum speed	170 mph (149 kt)	178 mph (155 kt)
Cruising speed	162 mph (141 kt)	167 mph (145 kt)
Stalling speed	55 mph (48 kt)	56 mph (49 kt)
Initial climb	1,090 ft/min	1,010 ft/min
Service ceiling	19,600 ft	17,150 ft
Range	650 sm (42 gal)	470 sm (55 gal)

Cessna 182/Skylane

Cessna added the 182 to its product line in 1956 as a trigear, upholstered version of the 180. The Skylane version, which is to the 182 as the Skyhawk is to the 172, followed in 1958.

Essentially, the Skylanes are heavier (500–600 lb), more powerful (about 40 percent) versions of the Skyhawk; and though most other airplanes in this class have retractable landing gear, the Skylanes have traded the extra performance so gained for lowered maintenance and insurance costs and, by uncomplicating things, have given pilots one thing less to worry about. You cannot scoff at this trade-off, because too many buyers obviously agree with it. The twenty-thousandth Skylane was built back in 1975.

The Cessna Skylane is another very successful design that has changed little over the years. The 1964 version is shown.

So, the 182/Skylane is a high-performance personal/business airplane with its gear permanently down and locked. It has always used the same Continental O-470 engine of 230 hp that powers the 180, and it has received periodic improvements as have other Cessnas. The swept tail was added in 1960; an additional window appeared on each side the following year, and in 1962 the cabin width was increased and the big rear window appeared. The 1969 model had its main gear legs shortened and given a wider stance; the tubular steel gear legs came in 1972, along with the modified leading-

64

edge for the wing. In 1977, the Skylane was fitted with the Continental O-470-U engine, which, because of higher compression (100-octane fuel), achieves its 230 hp at 2,400 rpm, 200 rpm less than the previous O-470-S. The 1978 182/Skylane went to the 28-v electrical system.

These are cross-country airplanes. They have the speed, range, and low pilot-fatigue factor to make them so, and they are good IFR platforms, stable and with a heavy airplane feel.

Cessna 182/Skylane (1974)

Wing span	35 ft, 10 in
Length	28 ft, 2 in
Height	9 ft, 1.5 in
Empty weight	1,645 lb
Gross weight	2,950 lb
Useful load	1,305 lb
Wing loading	16.9 lb/sq ft
Power loading	12.8 lb/hp
Baggage capacity	200 lb
Maximum speed	168 mph (146 kt)
Cruising speed	160 mph (139 kt)
Stalling speed	57 mph (50 kt)
Initial climb	890 ft/min
Service ceiling	17,700 ft
Range (60 gal)	690 sm

The 1978 Skylane. More Skylanes have been built than any other Cessna except the 172/Skyhawks.

Interior of the 1978 Skylane.

The sporty Cardinal is unlike all other Cessnas. Pictured is a 1977 model.

Cessna 177/Cardinal

When Cessna announced the first 177/Cardinal late in 1967 (1968 model), they refused to say that it was intended as a replacement for the 172/Skyhawk. What they did say was that the Cardinal represented the "Cessna image of the seventies." It did not work out that way. True, it was the best-looking Cessna yet—low and sporty and sexy— but it did not "fly like a Cessna," and Cessnaphiles did not like that. It was just too sensitive. Instead of giving the mashed potato feel of Skyhawk ailerons, the Cardinal ailerons responded instantly. The plane's big stabilator was strong right into the flare on landing. If you had not been flying Cessnas, chances are you liked the new Cardinal.

Cessna picked up the tab for gentling the Cardinal. Inverted slots were added to the stabilator's leading edges and the control linkage was modified. The original 150-hp engine was replaced with a 180-hp O-360 Lycoming on the 1969 model, and the 1970 model appeared with a constant-speed propeller and modified wing leading edge—all of which has resulted in an excellent airplane (this writer would pick it over any other fixed-gear Cessna). But Cardinal sales have never equaled Cessna's expectations, and the Cardinal has taken no Skyhawk customers. Its buyers are a breed apart.

The retractable-landing-gear version of the Cardinal (described in the next chapter) entered the market in 1971.

Cessna 177/Cardinal (180 hp)

Wing span	35 ft, 6 in	Baggage capacity	120 lb
Length	26 ft, 11.5 in	Maximum speed	150 mph (130 kt)
Height	9 ft, 1 in	Cruising speed	139 mph (121 kt)
Empty weight	1,430 lb	Stalling speed	53 mph (46 kt)
Gross weight	2,500 lb	Initial climb	840 ft/min
Useful load	1,070 lb	Service ceiling	14,600 ft
Wing loading	14.4 lb/sq ft	Range (49 gal)	675 sm
Power loading	13.9 lb/hp		

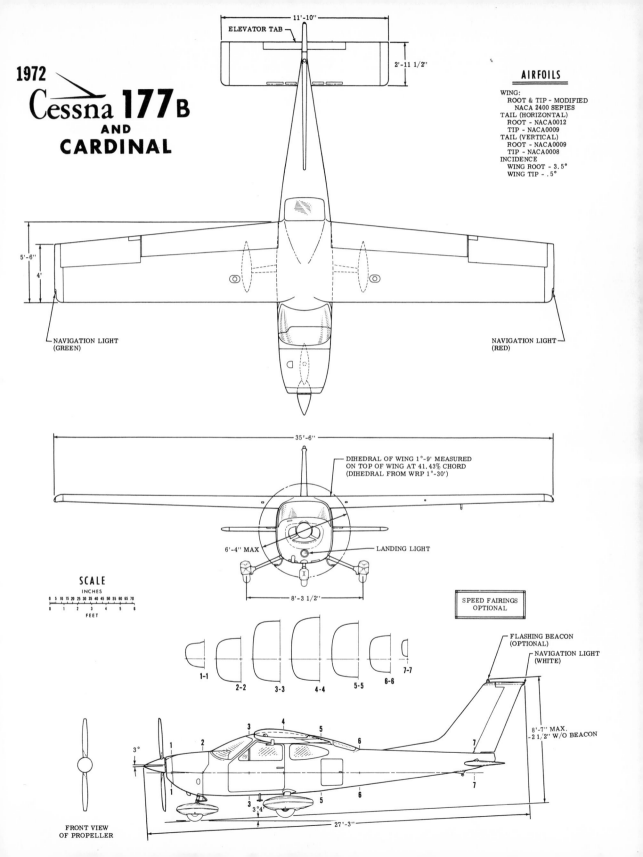

1972
Cessna 177B
AND CARDINAL

ELEVATOR TAB

11'-10"

2'-11 1/2"

AIRFOILS

WING:
    ROOT & TIP - MODIFIED
    NACA 2400 SERIES
TAIL (HORIZONTAL)
    ROOT - NACA0012
    TIP - NACA0009
TAIL (VERTICAL)
    ROOT - NACA0009
    TIP - NACA0008
INCIDENCE
    WING ROOT - 3.5°
    WING TIP - .5°

5'-6"

4'

NAVIGATION LIGHT
(GREEN)

NAVIGATION LIGHT
(RED)

35'-6"

DIHEDRAL OF WING 1°-9' MEASURED
ON TOP OF WING AT 41.43% CHORD
(DIHEDRAL FROM WRP 1°-30')

6'-4" MAX

LANDING LIGHT

8'-3 1/2"

SCALE
INCHES
0 5 10 15 20 25 30 35 40 45 50 55 60 65 70
0 1 2 3 4 5 6
FEET

SPEED FAIRINGS
OPTIONAL

1-1   2-2   3-3   4-4   5-5   6-6   7-7

FLASHING BEACON
(OPTIONAL)

NAVIGATION LIGHT
(WHITE)

8'-7" MAX.
-2 1/2" W/O BEACON

3°

1 2 3 4 5 6 7

3°
3°4'

27'-3"

FRONT VIEW
OF PROPELLER

The P-206 series Cessnas became Stationairs in 1972. Pictured is a 1974 model Stationair.

Cessna 205, 206, 207, and Stationair

Sorting out Cessna's Utiline series can be a bit confusing beyond the 180 and 185. First came the Model 205, produced in 1962–64, essentially a fixed-gear version of the 210C of the same period and a six-placer. It was replaced in 1965 by the P-206 Super Skylane, built from 1965 through 1971, in effect a fixed-gear version of the 210D Centurion.

Meanwhile, the U-206 model, produced from 1964 through 1971, was called the Super Skywagon until 1969, at which time the *Super* was dropped because the bigger model 207 was introduced that year and that would have logically made it the Super Duper Skywagon.

In 1972, this was all straightened out when Cessna dropped the 206 designations, replacing them with the Stationair, which continues in production, along with the 207 Skywagon.

These two stretched Cessnas use the same airframe, except that the 207 Skywagon is 3 ft, 6.75 in. longer. This extra length is inserted just ahead of the double cargo doors, which adds cubic feet to the cabin, and an extra window on each side, making this a seven-place airplane.

These airplanes received another name change in 1978. The Stationair (206 series) became the Stationair 6 and featured club seating. The Skywagon 207 became the Stationair 7.

The engines remain the Continental IO-520-F rated at 300 hp for takeoff, 285 hp continuous. The Model 205 had 260 hp.

The 206 series has been available with turbo supercharging since 1966, and the 207 series has had turbo supercharging since 1969; that is, the stretched Cessnas have been offered with and without turbocharging.

In sum, the Stationairs are primarily aimed at the charter, cargo, and air ambulance operators; they are aerial station wagons with good speed, range, and operating economy. The club seating offered with the 1978 Stationair 6 suggests that Cessna expects this craft to be used by business executives for medium and short distances.

If you are moving up from smaller Cessnas, the new controls to get used to are the auxiliary fuel pump, cowl flaps, prop control, and rudder trim. In flight, the stretched Cessna is a pussycat to handle. It lands like a Skylane; just hold the nose wheel off as long as possible.

Cessna 206, 207, and Stationairs

	P-206 (1970)	U-206 (1970)
Wing span	35 ft, 10 in	35 ft, 10 in
Length	28 ft, 3 in	28 ft
Height	9 ft, 7.5 in	9 ft, 7.5 in
Empty weight	1,835 lb	1,710 lb
Gross weight	3,600 lb	3,600 lb
Useful load	1,765 lb	1,890 lb
Wing loading	20.7 lb/sq ft	20.7 lb/sq ft
Power loading	12 lb/hp	12 lb/hp
Maximum speed	174 mph (152 kt)	174 mph (152 kt)
Cruising speed	163 mph (142 kt)	163 mph (142 kt)
Stalling speed	61 mph (53 kt)	61 mph (53 kt)
Initial climb	920 ft/min	920 ft/min
Service ceiling	14,800 ft	14,800 ft
Range (63 gal)	650 sm	650 sm

The original U-206-series Cessnas were Super Skywagons and Skywagons from their first appearance in 1964 until 1978, when the Skywagon 207 became the Stationair 7. Pictured is a 1974 Skywagon 207.

The 1978 Stationair 6.

	Stationair (1974)	Skywagon 207 (1973)
Wing span	35 ft, 10 in	35 ft, 10 in
Length	28 ft	31 ft, 9 in
Height	9 ft, 7.5 in	9 ft, 6.5 in
Empty weight	1,850 lb	1,900 lb
Gross weight	3,600 lb	3,800 lb
Useful load	1,750 lb	1,900 lb
Wing loading	20.7 lb/sq ft	21.8 lb/sq ft
Power loading	12 lb/hp	12.7 lb/hp
Maximum speed	174 mph (152 kt)	168 mph (146 kt)
Cruising speed	164 mph (143 kt)	159 mph (138 kt)
Stalling speed	61 mph (53 kt)	67 mph (58 kt)
Initial climb	920 ft/min	810 ft/min
Service ceiling	14,800 ft	13,300 ft
Range	650 sm (63 gal)	585 sm (58 gal)

The 1978 Stationair 7.

	Stationair 6 (1978)	Stationair 7 (1978)
Wing span	35 ft, 10 in	35 ft, 10 in
Length	28 ft, 3 in	31 ft, 9 in
Height	9 ft, 7.5 in	9 ft, 6.5 in
Empty weight	1,908 lb	2,095 lb
Gross weight	3,600 lb	3,800 lb
Useful load	1,704 lb	1,717 lb
Wing loading	20.7 lb/sq ft	21.8 lb/sq ft
Power loading	12 lb/hp	12.7 lb/hp
Maximum speed	178 mph (156 kt)	172 mph (150 kt)
Cruising speed	168 mph (147 kt)	164 mph (143 kt)
Stalling speed	62 mph (54 kt)	67 mph (58 kt)
Initial climb	920 ft/min	810 ft/min
Service ceiling	14,800 ft	13,300 ft
Range	510 sm (59 gal)	445 sm (54 gal)

Interior of the 1978 Stationair 6.

Interior of the 1978 Stationair 7.

The four-place Gulfstream-American Traveler was renamed the Cheetah in 1975. Its engine is the 150-hp Lycoming O-320.

Gulfstream-American Traveler, Cheetah, and Tiger

The four-place Gulfstream-American Traveler, an inevitable follow-up to the two-place Yankee, entered the market late in 1971 powered with the 150-hp Lycoming O-320 engine and was clearly aimed at the Skyhawk and Cherokee market, but it was a very different kind of airplane. It certainly looked different; compact and sporty, the Traveler did have more spirit and required that its pilots pay attention. Controls were sensitive, including trim, and landings were definite, with no float. In other words, this airplane, and its successors, the Cheetah and Tiger, are not going to provide all that margin for careless or inept handling that the gentle Skyhawks and Cherokees offer. If you prefer to fly the airplane rather than have it fly you, you will probably like these little craft.

The Tiger model has 180 hp and a corresponding increase in performance. Meanwhile, late in 1975, the Traveler was renamed the Cheetah after being given a larger stabilizer and a little more flap area.

The Traveler/Cheetah and the Tiger have no rivets; their metal skin is heat-bonded to structural members made of aluminum honeycomb. This results in a smoother exterior surface, which reduces drag, but it does cause one to wonder about repair costs. Normal maintenance costs are low.

Gulfstream-American Traveler/Cheetah and Tiger

	Traveler (1973)	Tiger (1975)
Wing span	31 ft, 6 in	31 ft, 6 in
Length	22 ft	22 ft
Height	8 ft	8 ft
Empty weight	1,200 lb	1,285 lb
Gross weight	2,200 lb	2,400 lb
Useful load	1,000 lb	1,115 lb
Wing loading	15.7 lb/sq ft	17.1 lb/sq ft
Power loading	14.7 lb/hp	13.3 lb/hp
Baggage capacity	120 lb	120 lb
Maximum speed	150 mph (130 kt)	170 mph (148 kt)
Cruising speed	140 mph (122 kt)	160 mph (139 kt)
Stalling speed	58 mph (51 kt)	61 mph (53 kt)
Initial climb	660 ft/min	850 ft/min
Service ceiling	12,650 ft	14,600 ft
Range	600 sm (38 gal)	765 sm (52 gal)

The Maule M-5 Rocket is a simple STOL airplane designed for short-field and unimproved-field operations. It has no complex aerodynamic devices to achieve this purpose (or raise maintenance costs); it does it with an efficient wing and a power loading that would sound good for an unlimited aerobatic airplane. The wing, by the way, is all-metal; the fuselage is tubular steel covered with fiberglass cloth.

The first Maule, which appeared in 1962, had 145 hp. Then, B. D. Maule, who builds these craft in Moultrie, Georgia, upped this to 210 hp in 1965 with the M-4 model. In 1967, the Franklin-powered M-4 went to 220 hp, a 180-hp version was offered in 1970, and in 1975 the first M-5 model was fitted with a 210-hp Continental engine. Finally, in 1976, the M-5 was equipped with the derated O-540-J Lycoming of 235 hp. With this engine, landings and takeoffs in still air and fully loaded may be accomplished in 350 ft, or 550 ft over a 50-ft obstacle.

Maule M-4 and M-5 Rocket

Maule M-5 (220 hp and 235 hp)

	M-5, 220 hp (1975)	M-5, 235 hp (1976)
Wing span	30 ft, 10 in	30 ft, 10 in
Length	22 ft	23 ft
Height	6 ft, 2 in	6 ft, 2 in
Empty weight	1,350 lb	1,400 lb
Gross weight	2,300 lb	2,300 lb
Useful load	950 lb	900 lb
Wing loading	15.1 lb/sq ft	15.1 lb/sq ft
Power loading	10.4 lb/hp	9.8 lb/hp
Cruising speed	165 mph (144 kt)	170 mph (148 kt)
Stalling speed	37 mph (32 kt)	40 mph (35 kt)
Initial climb	1,250 ft/min	1,500 ft/min
Service ceiling	19,000 ft	25,000 ft
Range (42 gal)	600 sm	457 sm

The Maule has unusual short-field performance.

Leave it to ex-military pilots to give you a good formation shot. Here, the Piper Tri-Pacer is boxed by a Super Cub and Apache in this 1955 photo.

Piper Pacer PA-20 and Tri-Pacer PA-22

The Piper Pacer, built from 1950 to 1952 inclusive, evolved from the two-place Vagabond of 1948, by way of the 1949 PA-16 Clipper. These were the first four-place Pipers.

The Pacer is a typical Piper of that period—metal-framed, fabric-covered, and easy to fly. The Pacers are taildraggers. The first ones were powered with the O-235 Lycoming of 115 hp and priced at $3,795. However, most Pacers were fitted with the Lycoming O-290D of 125 hp. The 1952 Pacers were equipped with the O-290D2, rated at 135 hp, but few were built before production halted in 1953 because the trigear version of the Pacer, the PA-22 Tri-Pacer, introduced in 1952, was claiming most of the sales.

The Piper Tri-Pacer remained in production throughout the fifties. Early models were equipped with the O-290D engine, then the O-290D2. By 1959, the Caribbean model was powered with the Lycoming O-320 of 150 hp, while the Standard and Super Custom models were fitted with the Lycoming O-320-B rated at 160 hp.

The Tri-Pacers are metal-framed and fabric-covered. The 1959 Caribbean sold new for $8,395. The deluxe version of the Caribbean cost an additional $1,000 and possessed a 12-channel Narco Superhomer, nav lights, wheel fairings, strut cuffs, and attitude gyro. The 160-hp model had a base price of $8,890, while the Super Custom 160-hp model, with radios and full panel, was priced at $10,770.

The Piper Pacer was a real beauty that cruised faster and looked better than its little brother, the Tri-Pacer. But, alas, the day of the tail wheel on the nose had arrived and the public had to have it. *Courtesy of Don Eiler's Custom Photography.*

The Tri-Pacer's cabin is functional. The vertical handle beneath the instrument panel is the brake lever.

The 1966 Piper Cherokee 235.

Piper Pacer PA-20 and Tri-Pacer PA-22

	PA-20 (125 hp)	PA-22 (150 hp)
Wing span	29 ft, 4 in	29 ft, 4 in
Length	20 ft, 5 in	20 ft, 5 in
Height	6 ft, 4.5 in	8 ft, 4 in
Empty weight	970 lb	1,100 lb
Gross weight	1,800 lb	2,000 lb
Useful load	830 lb	900 lb
Wing loading	12.2 lb/sq ft	13.5 lb/sq ft
Power loading	14.4 lb/hp	13.3 lb/hp
Baggage capacity	50 lb	100 lb
Maximum speed	135 mph (117 kt)	137 mph (119 kt)
Cruising speed	125 mph (109 kt)	123 mph (107 kt)
Stalling speed	48 mph (43 kt)	48 mph (43 kt)
Initial climb	810 ft/min	725 ft/min
Service ceiling	14,250 ft	15,500 ft
Range (36 gal)	580 sm	500 sm

**Piper
Cherokee
PA-28,
Models 140–180
and Archer;
Warrior**

The first Cherokee, the four-place, 150-hp Model 140, was introduced late in 1960, and this craft has remained in production, variously known over the years as the 140, 140B, Flite Liner, and Cruiser. Piper regards it as a two- to four-place airplane.

Beginning with the 1964 models, the Cherokee was also offered with 160 hp, 180 hp, and 235 hp. These aircraft have remained in production with yearly detail improvements and, until 1972–73, were designated the Cherokee Cs and Ds. That is, the 1968–71 models included, for example, the 180D and 235C.

Meanwhile, the Cherokee Six PA-32 was added to the tribe in 1966.

From 1972, these same-horsepower-class Cherokees have continued, but at that time Piper began giving them new names and some redesign. In 1972 the Cherokees received a redesigned rudder, plus a dorsal fin, and the 140 became the Cruiser, while the 180D and 235C and Cherokee Six (by then seating seven) filled out the line.

In 1973, when the new 150-hp Warrior was introduced, the 180D became the Archer and the 235C was renamed the Charger. In 1974, the Charger 235 became the Pathfinder 235, and in 1976 the Archer 180 received the Warrior's tapered wing to become the Archer II.

The Warrior wing is the most significant development among the fixed-gear Cherokees since their inception. The Frise ailerons, each 100 in. long, provide an aileron response that the Cherokee wing previously lacked. The Warrior wing tapers outboard of the flaps and is 5 ft longer than earlier Cherokee wings. It has the same area as the earlier wings, but the greater aspect ratio of the tapered portion reduces drag while providing just as much lift. The airfoil shape is modified near the tips, and the angle of incidence for the entire wing decreases 3° from root to tip, forcing the stall to progress outward from the roots.

This wing, mated to the 180 fuselage (three windows on each side and a wider cabin than that of the 140s) and powered with the 140's engine of 150 hp, made the Warrior. The Cherokee Warrior, of course, is meant to compete directly with the Cessna Skyhawk and the Gulfstream-American Cheetah.

Cherokee 140C, Warrior, 180D, and Archer 180

	140C (150 hp)	**Warrior (150 hp)**
Wing span	30 ft	35 ft
Length	23 ft, 4 in	23 ft, 9 in
Height	7 ft, 4 in	7 ft, 4 in
Empty weight	1,210 lb	1,301 lb
Gross weight	2,150 lb	2,325 lb
Useful load	940 lb	1,024 lb
Wing loading	13.4 lb/sq ft	13.67 lb/sq ft
Power loading	14.3 lb/hp	15.5 lb/hp
Baggage capacity	200 lb	200 lb
Maximum speed	144 mph (125 kt)	135 mph (117 kt)
Cruising speed	135 mph (117 kt)	133 mph (115 kt)
Stalling speed	54 mph (47 kt)	58 mph (51 kt)

Possessing a new wing, the Cherokee Warrior appeared in 1973.

Initial climb	690 ft/min	650 ft/min
Service ceiling	14,900 ft	12,700 ft
Range (50 gal)	725 sm	690 sm

	180D (180 hp)	Archer 180 (180 hp)
Wing span	30 ft	32 ft
Length	23 ft, 6 in	24 ft
Height	7 ft, 4 in	7 ft, 10 in
Empty weight	1,230 lb	1,390 lb
Gross weight	2,400 lb	2,450 lb
Useful load	1,170 lb	1,060 lb
Wing loading	15 lb/sq ft	14.4 lb/sq ft
Power loading	13.3 lb/hp	13.6 lb/hp
Baggage capacity	200 lb	200 lb
Maximum speed	152 mph (132 kt)	148 mph (129 kt)
Cruising speed	144 mph (125 kt)	141 mph (122 kt)
Stalling speed	57 mph (50 kt)	61 mph (53 kt)
Initial climb	750 ft/min	725 ft/min
Service ceiling	16,400 ft	14,150 ft
Range (50 gal)	725 sm	725 sm

Piper Cherokee 235 and Pathfinder

The Cherokee 235—called the Pathfinder beginning with the 1974 model—first appeared in 1963. The early ones used the same airframe as the lower-powered Cherokees, except for 2 ft of extra wing span with heavier spars, along with the cabin and tailcone structures beefed up with heavier skins and stiffeners. Its engine is the Lycoming O-540-B2B5.

The 1973 Model 235 had its fuselage stretched a little, which improved appearance and added 5 in. in the cabin; and a new dorsal fin further enhanced its looks, while providing additional yaw stability. A constant-speed propeller was an optional item on these craft, but most seem to have one.

The 235 Cherokees are honest-to-goodness four-place airplanes that will carry a load equal to their own empty weights—that is, four big people, all their luggage, and full fuel tanks. These airplanes fly very much like all Cherokees except that you do of course notice the additional power and you go to the rudder trim each time you change power settings.

Maintenance costs are comparatively low on Cherokees, and although the earlier ones suffered from leaking fuel tanks, those have probably all been properly sealed by now.

Piper Cherokee Six 260, 300, PA-32

The Cherokee Six is Piper's aerial station wagon. The list price of the 300-hp version is approximately the same as that of Cessna's Stationair 7, but although the Stationair is a little faster and carries a greater load the same distance, the Cherokee Six is a nimbler machine: it gets off the ground

Piper Cherokee 235 and Pathfinder

	Model 235 (1968)	Pathfinder (1975)
Wing span	32 ft	32 ft
Length	23 ft, 6 in	24 ft, 2 in
Height	7 ft, 2 in	7 ft, 8 in
Empty weight	1,410 lb	1,550 lb
Gross weight	2,900 lb	3,000 lb
Useful load	1,490 lb	1,450 lb
Wing loading	17 lb/sq ft	17.6 lb/sq ft
Power loading	12.4 lb/sq ft	12.8 lb/sq ft
Baggage capacity	200 lb	200 lb
Maximum speed	166 mph (144 kt)	161 mph (140 kt)
Cruising speed	156 mph (136 kt)	153 mph (133 kt)
Stalling speed	60 mph (52 kt)	65 mph (56 kt)
Initial climb	825 ft/min	800 ft/min
Service ceiling	14,500 ft	13,550 ft
Range (84 gal)	935 sm	915 sm

By 1974 the Cherokee 235 had become the Pathfinder.

better, climbs faster, and has a higher service ceiling. The difference is where you would expect it to be: the smaller and lighter Cherokee Six has lower wing and power loadings than the Stationair.

There is another difference. Although both the Stationair's Continental IO-520-F and the Six's Lycoming IO-540-C4B claim 300 hp, the Lycoming has 20 cu in. of additional zap, and that does make a difference, whatever the engine settings.

The Cherokee Six's cabin is 4 × 4 × 13 feet. It has a single door over the wing on the right side and a double cargo door (which may be operated as a single) on the left side near the rear of the cabin. There is a 22-cu-ft baggage compartment aft, and another of 8 cu ft forward, between the engine firewall and front of the cabin.

The Six handles "Cherokee easy" in flight, but one must develop some type of fuel management procedure to keep things in balance with the four tanks. Fuel must be drawn from one of the inboard mains during takeoff and landing. Many pilots take off and fly for an hour on the left main, an hour on the right main, 30 minutes on the left outboard, 30 minutes on the right outboard, and then back to the left main. Since there is no cross-feed system or aileron trim, you must do it something like this.

Most pilots agree that this airplane flies best when loaded; but because of the great flexibility in loading, you must watch the weight and balance figures closely.

The 260-hp version of the Cherokee Six offers a little less performance. However, as a family airplane, air ambulance, or charter craft, the Cherokee Six 260 could well be more practical than its more powerful sister. Its 0-540-E4B Lycoming is not fuel-injected, as the prefix of the engine designation reveals.

Piper Cherokee Six 260 and 300, PA-32

	Cherokee Six 260	Cherokee Six 300
Wing span	32 ft, 9 in	32 ft, 9 in
Length	27 ft, 9 in	27 ft, 9 in
Height	7 ft, 10 in	7 ft, 10 in
Empty weight	1,754 lb	1,818 lb
Gross weight	3,400 lb	3,400 lb
Useful load	1,646 lb	1,582 lb
Wing loading	19.5 lb/sq ft	19.5 lb/sq ft
Power loading	13.1 lb/hp	11.3 lb/hp
Baggage capacity	200 lb	200 lb
Maximum speed	164 mph (143 kt)	174 mph (152 kt)
Cruising speed	153 mph (133 kt)	168 mph (146 kt)
Stalling speed	63 mph (55 kt)	63 mph (55 kt)
Initial climb	775 ft/min	1,050 ft/min
Service ceiling	12,800 ft	16,250 ft
Range (84 gal)	890 sm	850 sm

Stinson Voyager 108-1 and Station Wagon 108-2

The Stinson Aircraft Corporation of Detroit, formed by pioneer pilot and designer Eddie Stinson in 1926 and acquired by AVCO (which also controlled Lycoming) during the early thirties, produced a great many civil aircraft prior to World War II, including trimotor airliners and the classic Stinson Reliant series, SR-7 through SR-10 ("Gullwings"). In 1939, the company entered the lightplane field with the 75-hp Stinson 105, followed by the Stinson 90 in 1940.

The post–World War II Stinson 108 series were the Voyagers and Station Wagons, powered with Franklin 6A4-150 and 6A4-165 engines of 150 hp and 165 hp, respectively. At least 5,000 were built before Piper bought the 108 design in 1948; but only a few Piper-Stinsons were built before production stopped in mid-1949. The last 108s sold for $6,484 f.a.f.

The Stinson 108s are metal-framed and fabric-covered. These aircraft are not numerous in the used market, but *Trade-A-Plane* usually lists a few. Their most unusual feature is built-in slots near the wings' leading edges that gentle the stall characteristics. The Franklin engine company is out of production at this writing, but parts are available. Make sure that you get a "heavy-case" Franklin engine if you purchase one of these craft.

The Stinson 108 is still as popular as its dwindling numbers will allow. The last ones were built by Piper in 1949.

Stinson 108-2 (165 hp)

Wing span	34 ft	Baggage capacity	100 lb
Length	25 ft, 3 in	Maximum speed	133 mph (116 kt)
Height	7 ft, 6 in	Cruising speed	130 mph (113 kt)
Empty weight	1,320 lb	Stalling speed	62 mph (54 kt)
Gross weight	2,400 lb	Initial climb	580 ft/min
Useful load	1,080 lb	Service ceiling	15,500 ft
Wing loading	15.5 lb/sq ft	Range (50 gal)	550 sm
Power loading	14.5 lb/hp		

5

Used Four/Six-Place, Single-Engine, Retractable-Gear Airplanes

The high-horsepower, single-engine, retractable-gear airplanes subordinate economy and ease of operation to speed. They cost more to buy, fly, and maintain than do the fixed-gear aircraft of lesser power. Most do trade a little performance for the added weight of some pilot or passenger comforts, but speed is their raison d'être, the one thing they have to offer in exchange for their higher costs and their demands for a higher degree of pilot proficiency. That is not to imply that a Bonanza or Centurion or Viking is difficult to fly or requires unusual skills, but simply that such craft need good management. Speed is a compressor of time, including pilot-reaction time. So, at higher speeds, you must think farther ahead of your machine.

Fuel consumption has always been important to pilots because it indirectly defines the limits of range and/or payload, these two considerations being largely interchangeable. During recent years, however, fuel economy has assumed a new dimension as petroleum shortages have forced up fuel costs and left us with the suspicion that the worst is yet to come. This has directed attention to the retractables possessing less horsepower than the top-of-the-line 285–300-hp aircraft. These airplanes—the Cherokee Arrow, Beechcraft Sierra, Cessna Cardinal RG, Rockwell Commander 112A, Mooney's Chaparral and Executive—all employ the same engine, the 200-hp Lycoming IO-360.

The IO-360 series (the prefix *I* means "fuel-injected") has a recommended TBO of 1,200 h, and overhaul currently costs about $4,000. We should add that this engine has been the subject of several AD notes; therefore, if you are contemplating the purchase of a used airplane so powered, make sure that these modifications have been accomplished.

Earlier, carburetored versions of this engine, the O-360 rated at 180 hp, have recommended TBOs of 2,000 h, and overhaul costs are in the $3,500–$3,600 range. The O-360 powers the Cherokee Arrow 180, Piper Comanche 180, Mooney Ranger, and Mooney Mk 21. These airplanes, in good condition, represent good buys in the used market, especially since depreciation will no longer be an important consideration in fixing their values.

There are also some "in-between" retractables with 225–260 hp that offer good performance at relatively modest cost. The 225-hp models of the Beechcraft Debonair (1960–70) are powered with the Continental IO-470-K, designed to operate on 80–87 octane fuel. These Debonairs will cruise at 160 kt, which is clearly more performance per dollar than the 285-hp Bonanza's 174-kt cruise.

Less numerous but regularly offered in the used market is the early 77

The Aero Commander 200 (Meyers) is faster than comparably powered Bonanzas but has a smaller cabin and 400 pounds less payload.

Cessna 210 (1960–63), fitted with the IO-470-E Continental of 260 hp. Here again, one may get a lot of performance for his money: an optimum cruising speed of 165 kt (190 mph) for less than $15,000.

There are some 1954–56 V-tailed E, F, and G35 Bonanzas in the marketplace with 225-hp engines (Continental E-225-8) and plenty of the H through P35 Bonanzas (1957–62) powered with the O-470 and IO-470 ranging in horsepower from 240 to 260. And although the V-tail's prestige (snob?) factor keeps the prices high on these airplanes, one does get back (presumably) the investment when one sells or trades.

As this is written, major overhaul of the E-225-8 engine costs about $3,200, $3,800 for the IO-470-K, and $4,800 for the IO-520 engines of 285–300 hp.

Recommended TBOs are 1,200–1,500 h for all. Fuel consumption at optimum cruise settings ranges from 9 gal/h for O-360 series engines to 16 gal/h for the IO-520s.

Aero Commander 200 (Meyers)

The Aero Commander 200 had a short production life during the sixties. (As this is written, the Meyers Aircraft Company, of Wheat Ridge, Colorado, has announced that they will return this airplane to production as the Meyers 200D.) About 50 of these airplanes were built during the early sixties as the Meyers 200, fitted with 240-, 260-, and 285-hp engines. Later, something less than 100 were built by the Aero Commander division of Rockwell International, after Aero Commander purchased the design in 1965.

The AC 200, which uses the same 285-hp Continental as the Bonanza, is

400 lb lighter than V-tails of the same vintage, and as much as 10 mph faster. It is also slightly faster than the newest Bonanzas and has an edge in climb rate and service ceiling.

However, the AC 200 pays for its "git-along" with a much smaller cabin and 400 lb less payload than a Bonanza. To get something, you have to give something.

In the used market, the AC 200 sells about $5,000 to $8,000 below Bonanzas of comparable age, equipment, and condition.

I can claim no direct experience with this airplane; but a friend who took one on a 1,500-m trip reports that it is stable and pleasant to fly, with the feel of a larger airplane. Elevator control is very effective at low airspeeds, although the rudder is not effective enough. Unusual torque/P-factor forces demand that the throttle be handled with respect, he reports. The adjustable front bucket seats are adequate for big people, but with big people in front there is not much leg room left for rear-seat passengers. Visibility is very good.

Aero Commander 200

Wing span	30 ft, 6 in	Baggage capacity	200 lb
Length	24 ft, 4 in	Maximum speed	212 mph (184 kt)
Height	7 ft, 4 in	Cruising speed	210 mph (182 kt)
Empty weight	1,985 lb	Stalling speed	54 mph (47 kt)
Gross weight	3,000 lb	Initial climb	1,450 ft/min
Useful load	1,015 lb	Service ceiling	18,500 ft
Wing loading	18.75 lb/sq ft	Range (82 gal)	1,060 sm
Power loading	10.5 lb/hp		

Beechcraft Bonanza Model 35 Series

The first Bonanza of 1947 had 165 hp and a wooden propeller.

79

Beech's V-tailed Bonanza has been in continuous production since its Approved Type Certificate was issued by the FAA (then Civil Aeronautics Agency) on March 25, 1947. Since so many have been built—about 14,000 to date, including the model 33s with the extra tail feather—I will sort them out by year, model, and engine installation.

1947–53: Models 35 and A35 through D35; E-185 Continental, originally rated at 165 hp maximum continuous, 185 hp for takeoff. Gross weight, 2,550–2,725 lb. Maximum cruise, 170–175 mph (149–152 kt).

1954–56: Models E35 through G35; E-225-8 Continental, 225 hp. Gross weight, 2,725–2,775 lb. Maximum cruise, 175–184 mph (152–160 kt). The E and F models were also available with the E-185 engine. The F model received some wing and tail beefing-up, along with a small third window on each side.

I should mention that the number and shape of Bonanza windows is not a reliable means of determining model, because so many older V-tails have been retrofitted with later-model windows.

Bonanzas prior to the H35 model burn 80 octane fuel.

1957: Model H35; Continental O-470-G, 240 hp. Gross weight, 2,900 lb. Maximum cruise, 170 kt (196 mph). Wing and tail structure further strengthened; heavier gauge skin on fuselage with closer rivet spacing. Minimum fuel grade, 91–96 octane.

1958–60: Models J35 through M35; Continental IO-470-C, 250 hp. Gross weight, 2,900–2,950 lb. Maximum cruise, 200 mph (174 kt). The first fuel-injected Bonanzas. Standard fuel capacity increased from 40 gal to 50 gal in the K35 model. The M35 was identical except for new "high-stability" wingtips.

1961–63: Models N35 and P35; Continental IO-470-N, 260 hp. Gross weight, 3,125 lb. Maximum cruise, 195 mph (170 kt). The third window was greatly enlarged beginning with the N35 model, and although power went up, so did gross weight, and performance suffered slightly. Optional 40-gal tanks in place of standard 25-gal tanks in each wing increased range. The P35 was produced in two years, 1962 and 1963.

1964–65: Model S35; Continental IO-520-B, 285 hp. Gross weight, 3,300 lb. Maximum cruise, 205 mph (178 kt). In addition to more power and increased useful load, the S35 model has a longer cabin to comfortably seat six. Baron-type third windows begin with this model, along with the "stinger" tail cone. This engine requires 100–130 octane fuel.

1966–67: Model V35 and V35TC (turbocharged); Continental IO-520-B, 285 hp, and TSIO-520-D, 285 hp, respectively. Gross weights, 3,400 lb. Maximum cruise, 203 mph (177 kt) and 230 mph (200 kt), respectively. The one-piece windshield distinguishes the V35 and the Bonanzas that followed, along with the fresh-air-intake scoop mounted atop aft fuselage.

Note: Since the Model 33 Debonair officially became a Bonanza in 1968, Beech decided that all V-tails would henceforth possess the *V* prefix in model designation. Therefore, instead of a W35 following the V35, the next one became the V35A.

1968–69: Model V35A and V35A-TC (turbocharged); Continental IO-

By 1964 the S35 Bonanza had 285 hp and six seats.

520-B, 285 hp, and TSIO-520-D, 285 hp. Gross weights, 3,400 lb. Maximum cruise, 203 mph (177 kt) and 230 mph (200 kt), respectively. Only minor detail changes from the previous model; whip-type ADF sense antenna in front of windshield removed, and instrument lighting changed from red to blue-white.

1970–78: Model V35B and V35B-TC (turbocharged); Continental IO-520-B, 285 hp, and TSIO-520-D, 285 hp. Gross weights, 3,400 lb. Maximum cruise, 203 mph (177 kt) and 230 mph (200 kt), respectively. Mostly detail changes during the seventies. Antislosh fuel cells were added in 1970, and the cabin interior was redesigned in 1972.

Now, it seems that most of the airport lounge lizards—at least, those who have never flown a V-tailed Bonanza—are quick to mention this airplane's alleged proclivity to "hunt" or "fishtail" in turbulent air. This is because the V-tailed Bonanza has no vertical tail surface, they will assure you. I have spent a good number of hours in Bonanzas of the butterfly-tail persuasion and must report that one may detect a slight amount of oscillation in the yaw mode in rough air. It is no big deal. It also has little or nothing to do with the V-tail. Beech engineers will tell you that the oscillation is caused by the Bonanza's unusually low coefficient of drag, which provides a lesser overall dampening effect to stabilize turbulence-induced oscillation. Some point out that other aerodynamically clean aircraft, such as jet fighters—and the "straight-tailed" Bonanzas—share similar characteristics to a

Good airplanes that survive the test of time are like people: they tend to gain weight with age. The 1978 V35B Bonanza had a gross weight of 3,400 pounds, whereas the 1947 Bonanza grossed 2,550 pounds.

81

degree. As I said before, the aeronautical engineers get no free lunches; if you want to get something, you have to give something.

In smooth air, the V-tail is an aileron airplane, highly stable, especially in pitch trim. Control pressures are solid—amazingly so even in slow flight—and very well balanced. Bonanza landings are no problem as long as you keep your speed up; an over-the-fence speed of 70 kt (80 mph) seems just right. These airplanes are not going to float. Use full flaps under all conditions.

So, the V-tailed Bonanza is a lot of airplane. Quality oozes from every pore; and you cannot be exposed to one of these machines for long without being convinced that Beech means it when they say, "We'll let someone else build the cheapest airplanes possible; we'd rather build the best."

Beechcraft Bonanza, Models G35, M35, P35, and V35B

	G35 (1956)	M35 (1960)
Wing span	32 ft, 10 in	33 ft, 5.5 in
Length	25 ft, 2 in	25 ft, 2 in
Height	6 ft, 6.5 in	6 ft, 6.5 in
Empty weight	1,722 lb	1,832 lb
Gross weight	2,775 lb	2,950 lb
Useful load	1,053 lb	1,118 lb
Wing loading	15.3 lb/sq ft	16.4 lb/sq ft
Baggage capacity	110 lb	270 lb
Maximum speed	194 mph (169 kt)	210 mph (183 kt)
Cruising speed	190 mph (165 kt)	200 mph (174 kt)
Stalling speed	55 mph (48 kt)	59 mph (52 kt)
Initial climb	1,300 ft/min	1,170 ft/min
Service ceiling	19,000 ft	20,000 ft
Range	625 sm (40 gal)	700 sm (50 gal)

	P35 (1963)	V35B (1970)
Wing span	33 ft, 5.5 in	33 ft, 5.5 in
Length	25 ft, 2 in	26 ft, 4.5 in
Height	6 ft, 6.5 in	6 ft, 6.5 in
Empty weight	1,855 lb	1,960 lb
Gross weight	3,125 lb	3,400 lb
Useful load	1,270 lb	1,440 lb
Wing loading	17.27 lb/sq ft	18.8 lb/sq ft
Power loading	12.02 lb/hp	11.9 lb/hp
Baggage capacity	270 lb	270 lb
Maximum speed	205 mph (178 kt)	210 mph (183 kt)
Cruising speed	195 mph (170 kt)	203 mph (177 kt)
Stalling speed	60 mph (53 kt)	63 mph (55 kt)
Initial climb	1,150 ft/min	1,136 ft/min
Service ceiling	19,200 ft	17,500 ft
Range (50 gal)	650 sm	600 sm

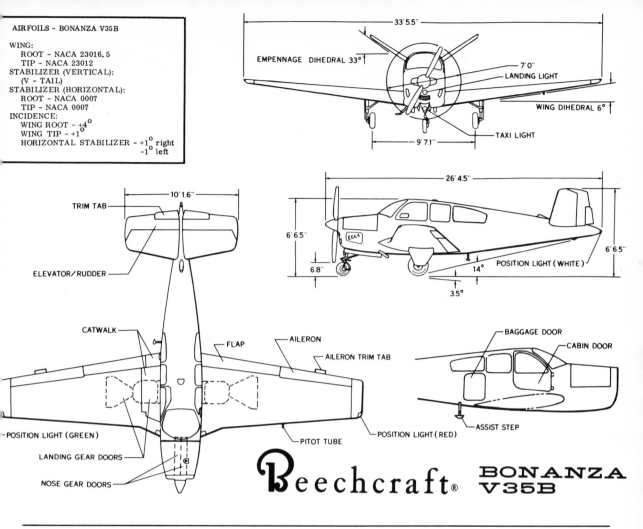

AIRFOILS - BONANZA V35B

WING:
  ROOT - NACA 23016.5
  TIP - NACA 23012
STABILIZER (VERTICAL):
  (V - TAIL):
STABILIZER (HORIZONTAL):
  ROOT - NACA 0007
  TIP - NACA 0007
INCIDENCE:
  WING ROOT - +4°
  WING TIP - +1°
  HORIZONTAL STABILIZER - +1° right
                    -1° left

Beechcraft BONANZA V35B

The Beechcraft Debonair, Model 33, was introduced in 1960 to compete with the Piper Comanche, which had appeared two years earlier, and the new Cessna 210, announced in 1959.

The 225-hp Debonair had a Bonanza airframe fitted with a conventional tail and lacked some of the V-tailed Bonanza's plushness. Priced at $19,995 for the standard airplane, it was $5,300 below the basic price of the M35 Bonanza, which came down the same assembly line.

The new Debonair was an excellent value (it outperforms the 250 Comanche), but customer acceptance was spotty. Only 1,600 Model 33s were built between 1960 and 1971.

Since the Model 33 has been in continuous production so long, I will sort it out as I did the V-tails above.

1960–67: Models 33, A33, B33, and C33 Debonairs; Continental IO-470-J and -K, 225 hp. Gross weights, 2,900–3,050 lb. Maximum cruise, 185 mph (161 kt).

Beechcraft Debonair/ Bonanza, Model 33 Series

83

The Beechcraft Debonair B33, 1963 model, gives a lot of performance on 225 hp.

The 1978 Bonanza F33A. Except for the extra tail feather, the Model 33 series has always employed the Bonanza airframe.

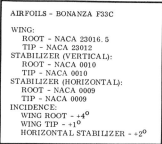

AIRFOILS - BONANZA F33C

WING:
    ROOT - NACA 23016.5
    TIP - NACA 23012
STABILIZER (VERTICAL):
    ROOT - NACA 0010
    TIP - NACA 0010
STABILIZER (HORIZONTAL):
    ROOT - NACA 0009
    TIP - NACA 0009
INCIDENCE:
    WING ROOT - +4°
    WING TIP - +1°
    HORIZONTAL STABILIZER - +2°

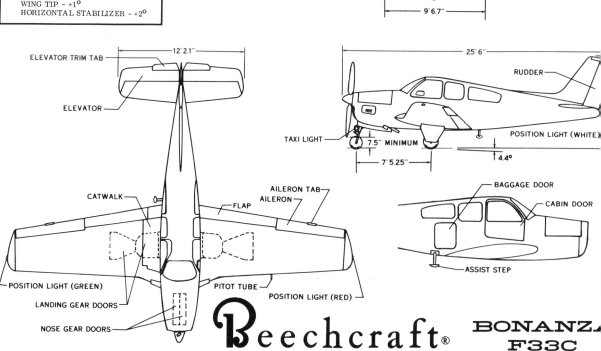

Beechcraft® BONANZA F33C

1966–67: Model C33A Debonair; Continental IO-520-B, 285 hp. Gross weight, 3,300 lb. Maximum cruise, 200 mph (174 kt).

1968–69: E33 Bonanza. Similar to C33 Debonair.

1968–69: E33A Bonanza. Similar to C33A Debonair.

1968–69: E33B and E33C Bonanzas. Aerobatic versions of the E33 and E33A, respectively.

1970: Model F33 Bonanza; Continental IO-470-K, 225 hp. Gross weight, 3,050 lb. Maximum cruise, 185 mph (161 kt).

1970–78 Model F33A Bonanza; Continental IO-520-BA, 285 hp. Gross weight, 3,400 lb. Maximum cruise, 200 mph (174).

1970: Model F33C Bonanza; aerobatic version of the F33A.

1972: Model G33 Bonanza; Continental IO-470-N, 260 hp. Gross weight, 3,300 lb. Maximum cruise, 193 mph (168 kt).

After flying a 1963 Debonair B33, I know why these machines are so much in demand in the used market. The clean Bonanza airframe does a lot with 225 hp—185 mph (161 kt) on 13 gal/h of 80 octane. This is, of course, essentially the same airplane as the 1970 F33 Bonanza except that the F33 burns 100 octane. The Bonanzas and Debonairs feel the same except that those with the conventional tail are a tad quicker on elevator and rudder response.

Bonanzas and Debonairs built prior to 1971 may be subject to momentary fuel starvation when the fuel is low and these craft are slipped, skidded, or rapidly turned on the ground unless antislosh fuel bladders have been retrofitted. This modification currently costs about $350.

Beechcraft Debonair/Bonanza, Models B33 and F33A

	B33 (1964)	F33A (1971)
Wing span	32 ft, 10 in	33 ft, 5.5 in
Length	25 ft, 6 in	26 ft, 8 in
Height	8 ft, 3.5 in	8 ft, 3.5 in
Empty weight	1,745 lb	2,056 lb
Gross weight	3,000 lb	3,400 lb
Useful load	1,255 lb	1,356 lb
Wing loading	16.9 lb/sq ft	18.8 lb/sq ft
Power loading	13.3 lb/hp	11.9 lb/hp
Baggage capacity	270 lb	270 lb
Maximum speed	195 mph (170 kt)	208 mph (180 kt)
Cruising speed	185 mph (161 kt)	200 mph (174 kt)
Stalling speed	60 mph (53 kt)	63 mph (55 kt)
Initial climb	960 ft/min	1,136 ft/min
Service ceiling	18,400 ft	17,500 ft
Range (50 gal)	625 sm	600 sm

Beechcraft Bonanza Model 36

The Model 36 Bonanza was introduced in June 1968. It was basically an E33A with 10 in. added to the forward cabin and with the fuselage moved 10 in. farther forward over the wing, while the aft bulkhead was moved rearward 19 in. to get 6 cu ft more cabin volume than possessed by the V35A. It is a full six-place airplane and can accommodate 170-lb passengers in all seats while remaining within its loading envelope.

The A36 model followed in 1970 and has remained in production since, accounting for half of all Bonanzas built in 1977. The A36 received a plushed-up interior after Beech discovered that its principal buyers were simply Bonanza owners who wanted more room, instead of the aerial workhorse operators the company expected to buy a stretched Bonanza. Models 36 and A36 use the same Continental IO-520-BA engine of 285 hp that powers the other late model Bonanzas.

Beechcraft Model 36

Wing span	32 ft, 10 in	Baggage capacity	400 lb
Length	26 ft, 4.5 in	Maximum speed	204 mph (177 kt)
Height	8 ft, 5 in	Cruising speed	195 mph (170 kt)
Empty weight	1,980 lb	Initial climb	1,015 ft/min
Gross weight	3,600 lb	Service ceiling	16,000 ft
Useful load	1,620 lb	Range (50 gal)	550 sm
Wing loading	20.2 lb/sq ft		
Power loading	12.6 lb/hp		

Beechcraft Musketeer Super R and Sierra 200

The Musketeer Super R, introduced in 1970, was an outgrowth of the 200-hp fixed-gear Musketeer Super, which had appeared in 1966. The Super R shared with the fixed-gear models a new fiberglass nose and a redesigned fuselage, which had a more rounded shape and gained 4.5 in. across the front seats. The Super R also has four windows on each side and space for two children's seats, which allows Beech to describe it as a four- to six-place aircraft. Its engine is the Lycoming IO-360-A2B, fitted with a constant-speed propeller.

Obviously aimed at the market proven by the very successful Piper Cherokee Arrow 200, Super Rs did not sell all that well and are not numerous in the used market. True, the Super R crowds the Arrow in performance, but the Arrow was priced about $5,000 below the Super R (basic airplane).

In 1972, Beech dropped the name *Musketeer,* and the Super R became the A24R Sierra. In 1973, the Sierra acquired a lighter control response when the stabilizer tab linkage was modified and received a new door for rear entry on the left side.

The Sierra 200, B24R, entered production in 1974 and went through recertification because of installation of a different engine, the Lycoming IO-360-A1B with counterbalanced crankshaft.

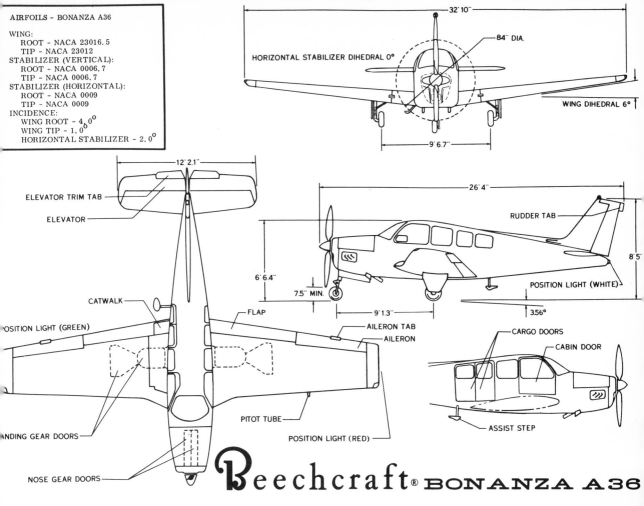

AIRFOILS - BONANZA A36

WING:
   ROOT - NACA 23016.5
   TIP - NACA 23012
STABILIZER (VERTICAL):
   ROOT - NACA 0006.7
   TIP - NACA 0006.7
STABILIZER (HORIZONTAL):
   ROOT - NACA 0009
   TIP - NACA 0009
INCIDENCE:
   WING ROOT - 4.0°
   WING TIP - 1.0°
   HORIZONTAL STABILIZER - 2.0°

32' 10"
84" DIA.
HORIZONTAL STABILIZER DIHEDRAL 0°
WING DIHEDRAL 6°
9' 6.7"

12' 2.1"
ELEVATOR TRIM TAB
ELEVATOR

26' 4"
RUDDER TAB
8' 5"
POSITION LIGHT (WHITE)
6' 6.4"
7.5" MIN.
9' 1.3"
3.56°

CATWALK
FLAP
POSITION LIGHT (GREEN)
AILERON TAB
AILERON
CARGO DOORS
CABIN DOOR
LANDING GEAR DOORS
PITOT TUBE
POSITION LIGHT (RED)
ASSIST STEP
NOSE GEAR DOORS

Beechcraft® BONANZA A36

Beechcraft Super R and Sierra 200

	Super R (1970)	Sierra 200 (1974)
Wing span	32 ft, 9 in	32 ft, 9 in
Length	25 ft, 1 in	25 ft, 8.5 in
Height	8 ft, 3 in	8 ft, 3 in
Empty weight	1,625 lb	1,711 lb
Gross weight	2,750 lb	2,750 lb
Useful load	1,125 lb	1,047 lb
Wing loading	18.84 lb/sq ft	18.84 lb/sq ft
Power loading	13.75 lb/hp	13.75 lb/hp
Baggage capacity	270 lb	270 lb
Maximum speed	170 mph (149 kt)	161 mph (140 kt)
Cruising speed	161 mph (140 kt)	151 mph (131 kt)
Stalling speed	63 mph (55 kt)	63 mph (55 kt)
Initial climb	910 ft/min	890 ft/min
Service ceiling	15,000 ft	14,300 ft
Range (30 gal)	410 sm	440 sm

By 1977 the six-place A36 Bonanza accounted for half of the total Bonanza production.

87

The Beechcraft Musketeer Super R appeared in 1970, fitted with a fuel-injected 200-hp Lycoming engine.

The Beechcraft Sierra 200 was introduced in 1974, following the A24R Sierra, which had replaced the Super R Musketeer in 1972.

Pioneer aircraft designer Giuseppe Bellanca produced the first commercial lightplane with retractable landing gear in 1937. After World War II, a four-place version of the earlier Cruisair appeared, powered with a 150-hp Franklin engine. A 190-hp model followed and, in 1957, the 200-hp Cruismaster. All were good performers, but built in relatively small numbers. Bellanca seemed something less than a good businessman.

Bellanca had retired to his farm when Northern Aircraft of Alexandria, Minnesota, bought the company in 1956. Northern built 104 Cruismasters in 1957 and 1958; then, in 1959, it changed its name to Downer Aircraft and introduced the Bellanca 260, followed by the 260A in 1962.

In that year, the present-day Bellanca Aircraft Corporation was formed to take over Downer's assets and continued production with the Bellanca 260B. In 1967, when a 285-hp engine was installed in the 260C airframe, the result was the Viking.

The Downer 260 much resembled today's Vikings except that the 260 had the traditional Bellanca triple tail (two small vertical stabilizers at each end of the horizontal stabilizer). That feature was dropped with the 260B, which also had a redesigned fuselage. The 260C that appeared in 1967 is almost identical to the 260B and is fitted with the same engine, the Continental IO-470-F of 260 hp. And these two craft shared almost identical performance figures with the earlier Downer 260.

However, I am not sure how much credence is due these figures. If we accept Bellanca's performance figures for the past dozen years, we have to believe that the 260-hp models are 16 mph faster than today's Super Viking. That is not all. Several years ago, I flew a brand-new Viking, N6654V, and the cruising speed check, at 9,500 ft, with 20 in. manifold pressure and 2,400 rpms, gave 164 mph IAS. Corrected, this came to 198 mph. At that time, Bellanca was claiming 206 mph at 75 percent and 8,000. Today, the Bellanca Super Viking book lists 187 mph maximum cruise. As Alice said, this gets curiouser and curiouser.

The 260-hp model is long out of production and scarce in the used market. Factory base price of the 260C was $22,950 in 1966.

One has a choice of engines with the Super Viking 300 series: Continental IO-520-K, rated at 300 hp for takeoff and 285 hp continuous; the Lycoming IO-540-G1E5, which is similarly rated; or the Lycoming fitted with Rajay turbosupercharger.

The Vikings have a tubular steel fuselage structure with Dacron cover. Wings are all wood—spruce spars, spruce and mahogany ribs, covered with mahogany plywood and resin-dipped. There has never been a mandatory AD note issued on the Bellanca wing, and Bellanca insists that it is stronger and more durable than metal. My favorite AI tells me that there has been some fuel tank leakage problems with some Vikings, but no other special maintenance headaches.

Bellanca Model 260 and Viking; Super Viking 300

Above: The Bellanca 260C, built from 1967 through 1968, is powered with the Continental IO-470-F of 260 hp.

Below: The Bellanca wing is all wood and is, Bellanca says, both stronger and lighter than metal. It is resin-sealed and plywood-covered.

Below right: The Viking led the way to more comfortable light aircraft interiors.

Bellanca Models 260C and Super Viking 300

	260C (1967)	Super Viking 300 (1974)
Wing span	34 ft, 2 in	34 ft, 2 in
Length	22 ft, 11 in	26 ft, 4 in
Height	6 ft, 4 in	7 ft, 4 in
Empty weight	1,850 lb	2,210 lb
Gross weight	3,000 lb	3,325 lb
Useful load	1,150 lb	1,115 lb
Wing loading	18.58 lb/sq ft	20.59 lb/sq ft
Power loading	11.5 lb/hp	11.7 lb/hp
Baggage capacity	186 lb	186 lb
Maximum speed	208 mph (184 kt)*	195 mph (170 kt)
Cruising speed	203 mph (176 kt)	187 mph (163 kt)
Stalling speed	62 mph (54 kt)	70 mph (61 kt)
Initial climb	1,500 ft/min	1,170 ft/min
Service ceiling	22,500 ft	17,000 ft
Range (60 gal)	1,000 sm	800 sm

*Bellanca-published figures gave 1967 Viking 300 a maximum speed of 211 mph and maximum cruise of 206 mph at 3,000 lb gross. Figures listed here for the 260C are those advertised by Bellanca in 1967. I was unable to verify.

The Cessna 210 was introduced in 1960, an all-new design, despite the fact that it looked like a retractable Skylane. Its Continental IO-470-E of 260 hp gave it a maximum cruise of 190 mph (165 kt) at 7,000 ft, and that should have allowed it to cut into the Bonanza-Comanche market substantially. However, sales averaged only 212 units per year between 1960 and 1974. During the middle and late seventies, Centurion sales began to average over 500 units per year.

Known as the 210 during its first four years in the market, Cessna's high-wing speedster became the Centurion in 1964 when it received a redesigned wing with more flap area, enlarged tail surfaces, and the IO-520-A Continental of 285 hp (the cut-down turtle deck and big rear window were added in 1962, along with 4 in. more of cabin width). In 1967, the lift struts disappeared and the Centurion got its full-cantilever wing.

But the strutless Centurions of 1967–68 had 3° dihedral, which gave them a serious case of the uglies in the eyes of most pilots. So, in 1969, the dihedral was reduced to 1.5°. The nose-wheel strut was shortened that year, and the chin housing for the nose wheel removed.

In 1970, the Centurion received a 25 percent bigger cabin to make it a six-place airplane, with new side windows extending almost half the length of the cabin, and the tubular steel main gear legs that had been proven on the Cardinal. The 1970 model also went to the IO-520-L engine, rated at 300 hp for takeoff, 285 hp maximum continuous.

The next noteworthy change in the Centurion came when an electric pump replaced the engine-driven hydraulic pump for landing-gear operation and eliminated a major maintenance headache on Centurions produced prior to 1972. Next, the 1976 model gained an 8-kt speed increase as the

Cessna Model 210 and Centurion 210

The 1962 Cessna 210 is fitted with the fuel-injected Continental engine of 260 hp and offers exceptional performance for the money.

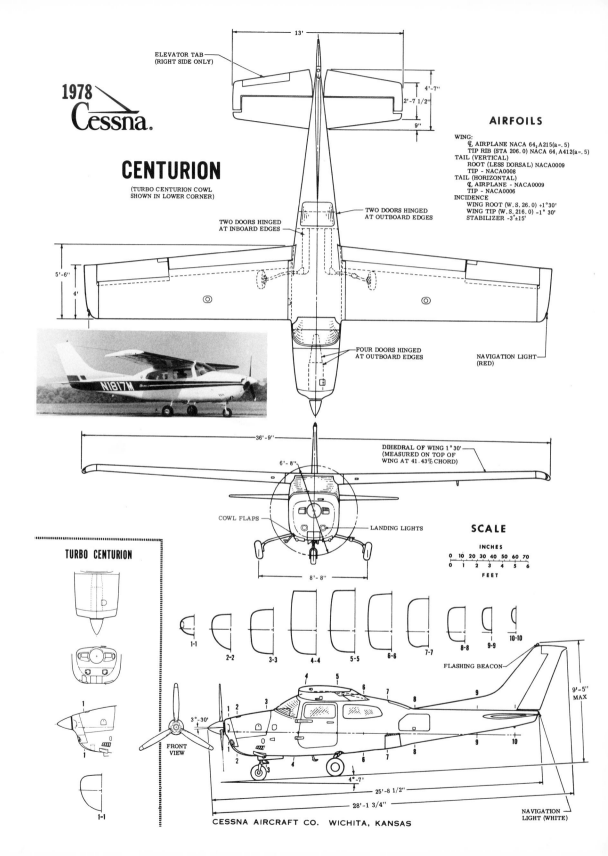

1978
Cessna®

CENTURION

(TURBO CENTURION COWL
SHOWN IN LOWER CORNER)

13'

4'-7"

2'-7 1/2"

9"

ELEVATOR TAB
(RIGHT SIDE ONLY)

TWO DOORS HINGED
AT OUTBOARD EDGES

TWO DOORS HINGED
AT INBOARD EDGES

5'-6"

4'

FOUR DOORS HINGED
AT OUTBOARD EDGES

NAVIGATION LIGHT
(RED)

AIRFOILS

WING:
  ℄ AIRPLANE NACA 64₂A215(a=.5)
  TIP RIB (STA 206.0) NACA 64, A412(a=.5)
TAIL (VERTICAL)
  ROOT (LESS DORSAL) NACA0009
  TIP - NACA0008
TAIL (HORIZONTAL)
  ℄ AIRPLANE - NACA0009
  TIP - NACA0006
INCIDENCE
  WING ROOT (W.S. 26.0) +1°30'
  WING TIP (W.S. 216.0) -1° 30'
  STABILIZER -3°±15'

36'-9"

DIHEDRAL OF WING 1° 30'
(MEASURED ON TOP OF
WING AT 41.43% CHORD)

6'-8"

COWL FLAPS

LANDING LIGHTS

8'-8"

SCALE

INCHES
0 10 20 30 40 50 60 70
0   1   2   3   4   5   6
FEET

TURBO CENTURION

1-1

2-2

3-3

4-4

5-5

6-6

7-7

8-8

9-9

10-10

FLASHING BEACON

9'-5"
MAX

FRONT
VIEW

3°-30'

4°-7'

25'-8 1/2"

28'-1 3/4"

NAVIGATION
LIGHT (WHITE)

1-1

CESSNA AIRCRAFT CO. WICHITA, KANSAS

result of the aerodynamic cleanup of some fairings and restyled fin and rudder tips. The 1977 and 1978 models received detail changes only, with the big news coming in 1978 with introduction of a pressurized version of the Centurion.

The Centurion is a big airplane, and a swift one. Throughout its production history its maximum cruise remained near 190 mph or better until the cleanup of the 1976 model raised this to 200 mph. During those years, it has gone from a 2,900-lb gross weight to 3,800 lb.

The Centurions have a large CG envelope to match their big cabins and great load-carrying abilities. Add to this a low pilot-fatigue factor, along with a 6–7 h range, and it is obvious that the Bonanza has more competition here than it really needs.

Cessna Model 210C and Centurion

	210C (260 hp, 1963)	Centurion (300 hp, 1978)
Wing span	36 ft, 7 in	36 ft, 9 in
Length	27 ft, 9 in	28 ft, 2 in
Height	9 ft, 9 in	9 ft, 5 in
Empty weight	1,780 lb	2,168 lb
Gross weight	3,000 lb	3,800 lb
Useful load	1,220 lb	1,644 lb
Wing loading	17.7 lb/sq ft	21.7 lb/sq ft
Power loading	15.3 lb/hp	12.7 lb/hp
Baggage capacity	200 lb	240 lb
Maximum speed	198 mph (172 kt)	202 mph (175 kt)
Cruising speed	189 mph (164 kt)	197 mph (171 kt)
Stalling speed	60 mph (53 kt)	64 mph (56 kt)
Initial climb	1,270 ft/min	950 ft/min
Service ceiling	15,000 ft	17,300 ft
Range	1,215 sm (65 gal)	1,005 sm (90 gal)

Interior of the 1978 Centurion.

The Cessna Cardinal RG entered the market in 1971, and a total of 904 were produced during the next five years. However, into the late seventies, sales of the retractable-gear Cardinal increased dramatically, and by 1978 the sporty Cessna with the tuck-away wheels was taking its share of the 200-hp retractable market. **Cessna Cardinal RG**

The Cardinal RG is a stable airplane in flight. It feels bigger than it is. Stabilator pressures are fairly heavy; ailerons are a bit lighter, and the rudder pedals feel as if they are attached to a big marshmallow. But stability and maneuverability are not compatible, and for the kind of flying the retractables do, a low pilot-fatigue factor is the important thing.

The Cardinal RG is a little heavier than its competition, but only the Mooneys (Chaparral and Executive) have a speed edge—which they pay for in useful load.

93

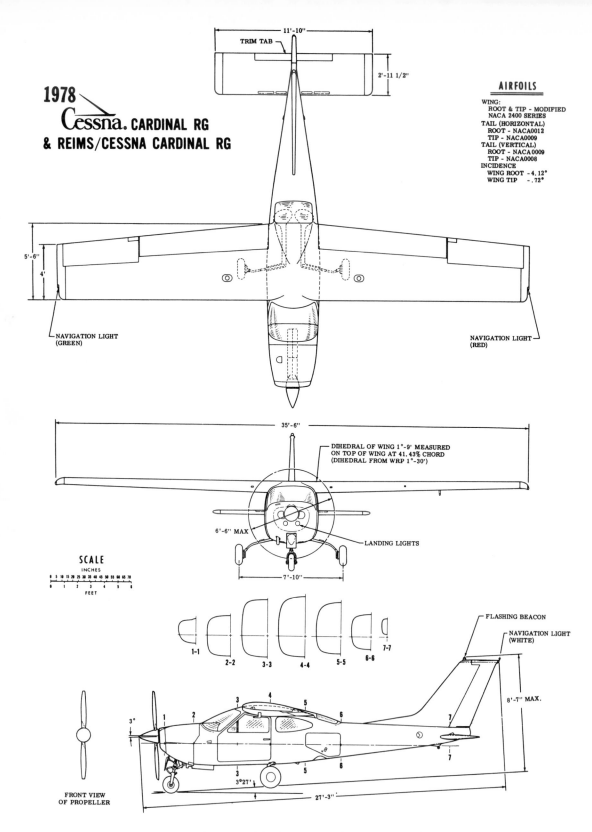

11'-10"

TRIM TAB

2'-11 1/2"

1978 Cessna. CARDINAL RG & REIMS/CESSNA CARDINAL RG

AIRFOILS

WING:
ROOT & TIP - MODIFIED
NACA 2400 SERIES
TAIL (HORIZONTAL)
ROOT - NACA0012
TIP - NACA0009
TAIL (VERTICAL)
ROOT - NACA0009
TIP - NACA0008
INCIDENCE
WING ROOT - 4.12°
WING TIP - .72°

5'-6"

4'

NAVIGATION LIGHT
(GREEN)

NAVIGATION LIGHT
(RED)

35'-6"

DIHEDRAL OF WING 1°-9' MEASURED
ON TOP OF WING AT 41.43% CHORD
(DIHEDRAL FROM WRP 1°-30')

6'-6" MAX

LANDING LIGHTS

7'-10"

SCALE

INCHES
0 5 10 15 20 25 30 35 40 45 50 55 60 65 70

0 1 2 3 4 5 6
FEET

1-1 2-2 3-3 4-4 5-5 6-6 7-7

FLASHING BEACON

NAVIGATION LIGHT
(WHITE)

8'-7" MAX.

3°

3°27'

27'-3"

FRONT VIEW
OF PROPELLER

CESSNA AIRCRCRAFT CO.   WICHITA, KANSAS

The Cessna Cardinal RG competes with the Cherokee Arrow and other 200-hp retractables.

Interior of the Cardinal RG.

The Cardinal RG stalls like a heavy Skyhawk. With the wheel all the way back, zero thrust, it bobs its nose and mushes but does not want to break clean with wings level. A brief check in a 1971 model confirmed that the book figures are honest. At 5,000 ft on a warm day (32° C/89° F), pulling 24 in. with 2,400 rpm, I trued-out at 169 mph (147 kt) lightly loaded.

The Cardinal RG's weird landing gear has less drag than most when extended; therefore, Cessna recommends that you simply leave it down during recovery from an aborted landing.

The 1972 RG received propeller blades with the Clark Y airfoil and that increased performance a little; the figures have remained constant since. The engine is the Lycoming IO-360-A1B6D.

Cessna Cardinal RG (1973)

Wing span	35 ft, 6 in	Baggage capacity	120 lb
Length	27 ft, 3 in	Maximum speed	180 mph (156 kt)
Height	8 ft, 7 in	Cruising speed	171 mph (149 kt)
Empty weight	1,660 lb	Stalling speed	57 mph (49 kt)
Gross weight	2,800 lb	Initial climb	925 ft/min
Useful load	1,140 lb	Service ceiling	17,100 ft
Wing loading	16.1 lb/sq ft	Range (61 gal)	945 sm
Power loading	14 lb/hp		

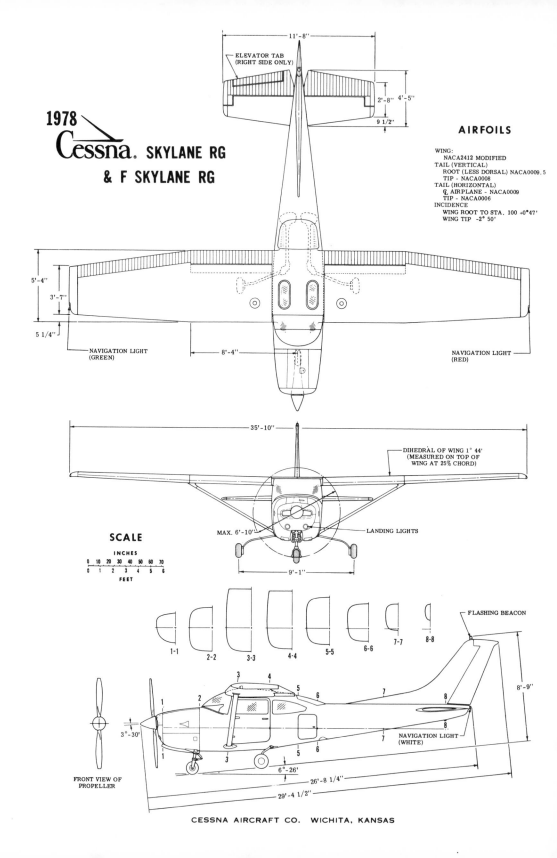

11'-8"

ELEVATOR TAB
(RIGHT SIDE ONLY)

2'-8" 4'-5"

9 1/2"

1978
Cessna. SKYLANE RG
& F SKYLANE RG

AIRFOILS

WING:
  NACA2412 MODIFIED
TAIL (VERTICAL)
  ROOT (LESS DORSAL) NACA0009.5
  TIP - NACA0008
TAIL (HORIZONTAL)
  ℄ AIRPLANE - NACA0009
  TIP - NACA0006
INCIDENCE
  WING ROOT TO STA. 100 +0°47'
  WING TIP -2° 50'

5'-4"

3'-7"

5 1/4"

NAVIGATION LIGHT
(GREEN)

8'-4"

NAVIGATION LIGHT
(RED)

35'-10"

DIHEDRAL OF WING 1° 44'
(MEASURED ON TOP OF
WING AT 25% CHORD)

SCALE

INCHES

0 10 20 30 40 50 60 70
0   1   2   3   4   5   6

FEET

MAX. 6'-10"

LANDING LIGHTS

9'-1"

1-1   2-2   3-3   4-4   5-5   6-6   7-7   8-8

FLASHING BEACON

8'-9"

3°-30'

NAVIGATION LIGHT
(WHITE)

FRONT VIEW OF
PROPELLER

6°-26'

6'-26'

26'-8 1/4"

29'-4 1/2"

CESSNA AIRCRAFT CO. WICHITA, KANSAS

The Cessna Skylane RG appeared in 1978, looking for all the world like a 1966 Centurion.

The Cessna Skylane with retractable landing gear entered the market in 1978, apparently to fill a pricing gap in the extensive Cessna line. I can think of no other reason for it, because it does not offer all that much ($13,000 worth) of extra performance over the fixed-gear Skylane, which has been so successful over the years. It does fill a price gap among Cessna single-engine retractables, because the base price of the Cardinal RG in 1978 was $43,950, and the plain vanilla Centurion was $63,950. The Skylane, at $49,950, fit nicely between. As this is written, it is too early to tell whether or not the retractable Skylane will find a significant market, and few will be in the used market for some time yet. It is my guess that it will still be rare five years from now. The engine is the Lycoming O-540-J3C5D of 235 hp.

Cessna Skylane RG

Cessna Skylane RG (1978)

Wing span	35 ft, 10 in	Maximum speed	184 mph (160 kt)
Length	29 ft, 4.5 in	Cruising speed	179 mph (156 kt)
Height	8 ft, 9 in	Stalling speed	58 mph (50 kt)
Empty weight	1,734 lb	Initial climb	1,140 ft/min
Gross weight	3,100 lb	Service ceiling	14,300 ft
Useful load	1,378 lb	(18,000 if optional	
Wing loading	17.8 lb/sq ft	EGT gauge is used	
Power loading	13.2 lb/hp	to set best power	
Baggage capacity	200 lb	mixture)	
		Range (56 gal)	595 sm

The Lake Buccaneer is a four-place amphibian that has been in production since the late fifties. Originally known as the Colonial Skimmer and built in Sanford, Maine, with an O-360 Lycoming for power rated at 180 hp, it is manufactured today by the Lake Division of Consolidated Aeronautics in Houston.

The modern Lake is fitted with an IO-360 Lycoming of 200 hp and offers good performance for an airplane that is equally at home operating from land or water. Lake engineers have managed to give this craft a very strong and efficient flying boat hull that does not significantly penalize speed, range, or useful load. Indeed, the Lake's advertised performance figures are

Lake Buccaneer LA-4-20

97

almost interchangeable with those of the Beechcraft Sierra, powered with a similar engine.

However, for the extra versatility, for the countless new and often remote places the Lake can take you to, there is a price—$8,000 more than a Sierra (new).

Lake Buccaneer LA-4 (180 hp) and LA-4-20 (200 hp)

	LA-4 (180 hp, 1966)	LA-4-20 (200 hp, 1975)
Wing span	38 ft	38 ft
Length	24 ft, 11 in	24 ft, 11 in
Height	9 ft, 4 in	9 ft, 4 in
Empty weight	1,555 lb	1,555 lb
Gross weight	2,400 lb	2,690 lb
Useful load	845 lb	1,135 lb
Wing loading	14.1 lb/sq ft	15.9 lb/sq ft
Power loading	13.3 lb/hp	13.45 lb/hp
Baggage capacity	200 lb	200 lb
Maximum cruise	132 mph (115 kt)	150 mph (130 kt)
Stalling speed	50 mph (43 kt)	45 mph (39 kt)
Initial climb	800 ft/min	1,200 ft/min
Range (55 gal)	528 sm	650 sm

Mooney Mk 20, Mk 21, Ranger, and Statesman

The modern Mooneys date from 1947, when Al Mooney and Charles Yankey formed Mooney Aircraft Company in Wichita to produce the single-place Mooney Mite. The company moved to Kerrville, Texas, in 1953, and two years later the 150-hp, four-place Mooney Mk 20 appeared. The Mk 20 had a wooden wing, a muscle-powered retractable gear, and a tail put on backward. But it was a lot faster than anything in its class—in fact, it was the only airplane in its class at that time. A total of 180 Mk 20s were built before it received the 180-hp Lycoming in 1958. The resulting Mk 20A had a maximum cruise of 180 mph. Anytime you can get a mile per hour for each horsepower in a four-place airplane, you are doing a lot of things right.

In 1960, Chief Engineer Ralph Harmon (Al Mooney left the company in 1959) transformed the Mk 20's wooden wing into metal to produce the Mk 21; and this airplane, with 180 hp, became the Mooney Ranger in 1967. A plushed-up version of the Ranger was the Statesman.

Also offered in the mid-sixties, with very limited success, was a fixed-gear version of the Mk 21, the Mooney Master, which could be converted to a retractable. I have not seen any in the used market.

No Mooneys were built during the early seventies following a brush with financial collapse in 1969 resulting from an attempt to market a single-engine pressurized model, the Mk 22 Mustang. Then, Mooney assets were acquired by Republic Steel Corporation, and production resumed early in 1974 with the 180-hp Ranger and the 200-hp Chaparral and Executive.

98

The early Lake amphibian had 180 hp; late models of the Buccaneer are fitted with 200-hp fuel-injected Lycomings.

The Mooney Ranger returns a 170-mph cruise for 180 hp.

The Mooney Chaparral of 200 hp.

The 1970 Mooney Executive 21, essentially a stretched Chaparral.

I flew a 1968 Ranger and liked it—once assured that the empennage was not attached to the airplane by way of a universal joint. Trim control, a wheel between the seats, tilts the entire tail unit, including the vertical surfaces and the tail cone. The tail is supported by heavy trunnions at the horizontal stabilizer spar and driven by a huge jackscrew. This eliminates trim tabs and their attendant drag.

You are also reminded that Mooneys are different when entering the cabin, because the first thing a Mooney owner will tell you is, "Don't slam the door." Just close it gently, and lock it with the forward-positioned handle. I would suggest that most other airplane makers study this mechanism.

Mooney controls are a little on the stiff side, partly because control surfaces are operated by push rods instead of wire cables. Also, all control surface hinge gaps are sealed, an aerodynamic nicety that adds its bit to speed and efficiency.

Mooney Ranger and Statesman

	Ranger (180 hp, 1968)	Statesman (180 hp, 1970)
Wing span	35 ft	35 ft
Length	23 ft, 2 in	24 ft
Height	8 ft, 4 in	8 ft, 4 in
Empty weight	1,525 lb	1,590 lb
Gross weight	2,575 lb	1,525 lb
Useful load	1,050 lb	935 lb
Wing loading	15.4 lb/sq ft	15.1 lb/sq ft
Power loading	14.2 lb/hp	14 lb/hp
Baggage capacity	120 lb	120 lb
Maximum speed	176 mph (154 kt)	174 mph (151 kt)
Cruising speed	170 mph (148 kt)	168 mph (146 kt)
Stalling speed	57 mph (49 kt)	61 mph (53 kt)
Initial climb	1,000 ft/min	1,100 ft/min
Service ceiling	19,500 ft	14,600 ft
Range (52 gal)	850 sm	810 sm

Mooney Super 21, Chaparral, Executive, and 201

The 200-hp Mooney Super 21 appeared in 1964, fitted with an IO-360 Lycoming. Produced through 1967, it employs the same airframe as the Mk 21. The Chaparral (M20E) is essentially the same airplane and possesses the same specifications and performance figures. The 1964 Super 21 will keep up with a 1974 Chaparral—and I should add that nothing else with 200-hp will keep up with either of them, except the new Mooney 201.

There is no question about it—the Mooneys get more suddenness per horsepower than anything. One reason for this is Mooney's ram air feature, an alternate air induction inlet on the front of the cowl that bypasses the air filter. It is sort of a poor boy's supercharger that boosts manifold pressure.

The Mooney 201 is a cleaned-up (aerodynamically) Mooney Executive, and the Executive is a Chaparral with the fuselage stretched 10 in. The model 201, introduced in 1977, will probably replace the other 200-hp Mooneys. The 201 has a new sloped windshield, the IO-360 with counterbalanced crankshaft, flush rivets, and a new cowl. Its interior is also the most luxurious ever offered by Mooney. But it still flies like a Mooney, and its tail is still on backward.

In sum, a Mooney offers the most performance for your dollar—an excellent airplane with poor dealer support.

Mooney Executive and Model 201

	Executive (1974)	Model 201 (1977)
Wing span	35 ft	35 ft
Length	24 ft	24 ft, 8 in
Height	8 ft, 4 in	8 ft, 4 in
Empty weight	1,640 lb	1,640 lb
Gross weight	2,740 lb	2,740 lb
Useful load	1,100 lb	1,100 lb
Wing loading	16.4 lb/sq ft	16.4 lb/sq ft
Power loading	13.7 lb/hp	13.7 lb/hp
Baggage capacity	120 lb	120 lb
Maximum speed	185 mph (161 kt)	201 mph (175 kt)
Cruising speed	177 mph (154 kt)	195 mph (170 kt)
Stalling speed	62 mph (54 kt)	61 mph (53 kt)
Initial climb	1,055 ft/min	1,030 ft/min
Service ceiling	18,800 ft	18,800 ft
Range (64 gal)	1,088 sm	1,208 sm

Navion and Navion Rangemaster

The Navion, powered with the Continental E-185-3 of 185 hp, was originally produced by North American Aviation (now a division of Rockwell International) in 1946 in anticipation of a postwar lightplane boom that never materialized. North American built 1,109 Navions before selling the design to Ryan Aeronautical Corporation. Ryan turned out 1,240 Navions, A and B models, fitted with E-185-9 Continentals (205 hp for takeoff) and GO-435-C2 Continentals (240 hp continuous, 260 hp for takeoff), respectively, from 1949 through 1951.

No Navions were built between 1951 and 1961. Then, the Navion Aircraft Corporation was formed in Seguin, Texas, to put this craft back into production. They reengined some of the earlier Navions with Continental O-470 and IO-470 series engines of 240 hp, 250 hp, and 260 hp. This company then marketed a brand-new Navion Rangemaster, powered with the Continental IO-470-H of 260 hp. Something over 120 Rangemasters were built, the last ones fitted with the Continental IO-520-B of 285 hp.

Finally, the Navion Rangemaster Aircraft Corporation of Wharton, Texas, resumed production with the Model H Rangemaster late in 1974; this airplane is fitted with the IO-520-13A engine of 285 hp.

101

Many of the older Navions have been reengined and otherwise modified, so that model or age means little. But a number of AD notes have been issued over the years on these craft's props, landing-gear linkage, fuel cells, and so on; therefore, if you are considering the purchase of a Navion, make sure that you have a mechanic familiar with Navions to check it out before you buy.

Navions are excellent short-field machines, are stable, and possess no unpleasant flight characteristics; but it is difficult to describe them in much detail, because performance varies with the many different engines to be found in them. Speeds range from 139 mph (121 kt) for the 185-hp versions to 157 mph (137 kt) for the fuel-injected 260-hp models to 191 mph (166 kt) for the 285-hp Rangemaster. An empty Navion will weigh anywhere from 1,700 to 2,100 lb, while the gross weight will vary from 2,750 to 3,315 lb.

Navions are equipped with a number of different engines, from 185 hp to 285 hp, and performance varies accordingly.

Navion B (1948) and Rangemaster (1970)

	Navion B (185–205 hp)	Rangemaster (285 hp)
Wing span	33 ft, 5 in	34 ft, 9 in
Length	27 ft, 8 in	27 ft, 5 in
Height	8 ft, 8 in	8 ft, 6 in
Empty weight	1,730 lb	2,000 lb
Gross weight	2,750 lb	3,315 lb
Useful load	1,020 lb	1,315 lb
Wing loading	14.6 lb/sq ft	17.6 lb/sq ft
Power loading	13.4 lb/hp	11.6 lb/hp
Baggage capacity	80 lb	190 lb
Maximum speed	157 mph (137 kt)	206 mph (179 kt)
Cruising speed	150 mph (130 kt)	191 mph (166 kt)
Stalling speed	54 mph (43 kt)	55 mph (44 kt)
Initial climb	900 ft/min	1,375 ft/min
Service ceiling	15,600 ft	21,500 ft
Range	500 sm (60 gal)	1,200 sm (108 gal)

Piper Comanche Models PA-24, 180, 250, and 260

The Piper Comanche entered the market in 1958 offering a choice of engines, the Lycoming O-360-A1A of 180 hp or the Lycoming O-540-A1A5 of 250 hp. The 180-hp Comanche was taken out of production in 1965, and buyers were given a different choice of engines, the O-540-E carburetored Continental of 250 hp or the fuel-injected IO-540-D of 260 hp. With an extra window added on each side, this craft became the Comanche B. A few Bs may have the 250-hp engine, but this option was discontinued in 1966.

In 1969, the Comanche C resulted when this airplane received a longer "shark" nose. The Comanche C, fitted with the same fuel-injected 260-hp engine as the B and a turbocharged version of the C, were produced until June 1972, when floodwaters destroyed Comanche tooling at Piper's Lock Haven, Pennsylvania, plant. Since Comanche sales were down to about 100 units per year at that time (1972 was bad for the entire industry), Piper decided against putting it back into production. Evidently, the Cherokee Lance, announced in mid-1976, takes the place of the updated Comanche many pilots hoped to see, although the Lance's true forerunner is the Cherokee Six.

Meanwhile, Comanches are much sought after in the used market. Most pilots regard the Comanche 180 as a bit underpowered, but a Comanche 250 or 260 will cruise at 180 mph (157 kt) or better, is good in slow flight, well mannered in stalls, and easy to land if you are not carrying too much speed. Fuel management is uncomplicated, and the Comanche has rudder trim, along with controls that are firm enough to make it easy to keep all your ducks lined up when on IFR.

The Comanche's cabin is rather austere; the stabilator trim is an overhead crank, and that misplaced joystick on the floor is the emergency landing-gear control. It stands up vertically when the gear is down and lies flat when the gear is up. It is fast and effective, however.

Standard fuel is a 30-gal main in each wing. Most Comanches have an additional 15-gal cell outboard in each wing, which gives an economy cruise duration of more than 10 h, or about 1,500 sm.

Piper Comanche PA-24-180 and PA-24-250

	Comanche 180 (1964)	Comanche 250 (1966)
Wing span	36 ft	36 ft
Length	24 ft, 8 in	25 ft, 3 in
Height	7 ft, 4 in	7 ft, 5 in
Empty weight	1,510 lb	1,630 lb
Gross weight	2,550 lb	2,900 lb
Useful load	1,040 lb	1,270 lb
Wing loading	14.3 lb/sq ft	15.7 lb/sq ft
Power loading	14.2 lb/hp	11.2 lb/hp
Baggage capacity	120 lb	200 lb
Maximum speed	167 mph (145 kt)	190 mph (165 kt)
Cruising speed	160 mph (139 kt)	181 mph (157 kt)
Stalling speed	62 mph (53 kt)	62 mph (53 kt)
Initial climb	910 ft/min	1,350 ft/min
Service ceiling	18,500 ft	20,000 ft
Range	1,100 sm (60 gal)	1,108 sm (90 gal)

The Piper Comanche PA-24 is fitted with engines of 180, 250, 260, and 400 hp. The 250/260-hp models are the best buys.

Piper Cherokee Arrow PA-28R, 180, 200, Arrow II, and Arrow III

The Cherokee PA-28R Arrow entered production in 1967, powered with the Lycoming IO-360, rated at 180 hp, and featuring its now famous and much-debated automatic landing-gear retract system. The Arrow was a full 20 mph faster than the fixed-gear Cherokee 180. Employing the same airframe, the Arrow grossed 100 lb more, used the Cherokee 235 stabilator (10 in. greater span), and had an "airliner-type" power quadrant and an extra window on each side.

The Arrow's most revolutionary feature was its stupid-proof landing-gear system. Some pilots still deride it, but it is pretty hard to argue with success. The landing-gear muscle is hydraulic by way of an electric pump; and the wheels go up and down automatically at the command of a sensing device mounted on the left side of the fuselage that measures differential air pressure. It causes the wheels to be lowered when airspeed falls below 105 mph (92 kt). It allows the gear to come up only after airspeed reaches 85 mph (74 kt) with full throttle at sea level. The system has a manual override selector switch mounted between the front seats that allows you to cork the gear-genie in his bottle.

The Arrow 200 appeared in 1969. Outwardly the only noticeable difference between it and the Arrow 180 is an additional air scoop on the right-hand side of the cowling. This is Piper's "automatic" oil cooler, which obviates the need for cowl flaps—and cowl-flap management. Under the cowl, there is another difference, the 200-hp Lycoming IO-360-C1C, which is why the oil cooler is necessary. The extra 20 hp does show up in the Arrow 200's performance figures.

The Arrow II, which appeared in 1972, is actually 5 in. longer than previous Arrows, and this turns up as more leg room in the rear seat. The Arrow II also has a bigger door, 26 in. more wing span, and the stabilator from the Cherokee Six. The extra structure added 65 lb to empty weight and eroded performance slightly; but the Arrow II is bigger and roomier, and with no increase in power it will still cruise at 165 mph (143 kt) on 10 gal/h.

The Arrow II's handling characteristics are no different from those of its predecessors, which is to say that the plane has no idiosyncrasies, no surprises—a proper machine that does everything correctly, if a bit dully. This, of course, is its strength. Arrow buyers—and there continue to be plenty of them—are looking not for a tiger but for an honest aerial vehicle with a nice balance between performance and economy.

The Arrow III appeared in 1977 equipped with the Cherokee Warrior wing—that is, the tapered wing that had been proven on the Warrior. This allowed a fuel capacity increase of 16 gal, shortened the landing roll, and upped the useful load.

Cherokee Arrow 200.

Piper Arrow 180, Arrow 200, Arrow II, and Arrow III

	Arrow 180 (1967)	Arrow 200 (1969)
Wing span	30 ft	30 ft
Length	24 ft, 3 in	24 ft, 3 in
Height	8 ft	8 ft
Empty weight	1,510 lb	1,450 lb
Gross weight	2,500 lb	2,600 lb
Useful load	990 lb	1,150 lb
Wing loading	15.6 lb/sq ft	16.3 lb/sq ft
Power loading	13.89 lb/hp	13 lb/hp
Baggage capacity	200 lb	200 lb
Maximum speed	165 mph (144 kt)	176 mph (153 kt)
Cruising speed	160 mph (139 kt)	166 mph (144 kt)
Stalling speed	62 mph (53 kt)	64 mph (56 kt)
Initial climb	850 ft/min	910 ft/min
Service ceiling	16,000 ft	16,000 ft
Range (50 gal)	830 sm	810 sm

	Arrow II (1972)	Arrow III (1978)
Wing span	32 ft, 2 in	35 ft, 5 in
Length	24 ft, 7 in	24 ft, 8 in
Height	8 ft	7 ft, 10 in
Empty weight	1,515 lb	1,754 lb
Gross weight	2,650 lb	2,750 lb
Useful load	1,135 lb	996 lb
Wing loading	15.59 lb/sq ft	16.18 lb/sq ft
Power loading	13.25 lb/hp	13.75 lb/hp
Baggage capacity	200 lb	200 lb
Maximum speed	175 mph (152 kt)	175 mph (152 kt)
Cruising speed	165 mph (144 kt)	165 mph (144 kt)
Stalling speed	64 mph (56 kt)	64 mph (56 kt)
Initial climb	900 ft/min	831 ft/min
Service ceiling	15,000 ft	16,200 ft
Range	750 sm (48 gal)	1,100 sm (72 gal)

The Cherokee Arrow II, which appeared in 1972, is five inches longer than previous Arrows, which shows up as more rear-seat leg room.

Piper Lance and Lance II

The Cherokee Lance was introduced in 1976 as a six- to seven-place high-performance retractable. With power equal to that of the Bonanza A36 or Centurion, the Lance trades some speed for a truly spacious cabin and the ability to haul nearly 1,300 lb up to 1,200 mi. I am tempted to describe the Lance as a cleaned-up Cherokee Six 300 with a retractable gear, but that would not be too accurate. The Lance is more airplane.

The 1978 Lance II more clearly defined the differences with its distinctive T-tail. Placing the horizontal tail near the top of the vertical tail and out of the propeller slipstream is said to improve pitch stability during landing-gear and flap operation, but it also requires a heavier supporting structure in the vertical tail, and its true advantage on propeller-driven airplanes is probably more aesthetic than aerodynamic.

The Lances have a heavy, solid feeling in flight, and control response is on the slow side. They are uncomplicated for their size and offer true passenger comfort for long flights. The engine is the Lycoming IO-540 of 300 hp, which has a 2,000-h TBO and an average fuel-consumption rate of 15–17 gal/h.

Piper Lance II

Wing span	32 ft, 10 in	Useful load	1,375 lb
Length	27 ft, 8 in	Wing loading	20.6 lb/sq ft
Height	9 ft, 6 in	Power loading	12 lb/hp
Empty weight	2,225 lb (fully equipped)	Baggage capacity	200 lb
Gross weight	3,600 lb	Maximum speed	190 mph (165 kt)

Republic Seabee, Model RC-3

Republic Aviation Corporation of Farmingdale, New York, builder of the famed World War II Thunderbolt and the later F-105 Thunderchief, among other things, tried the lightplane market immediately after the war with the Seabee. The Seabee is a four-place amphibian of pusher configuration, powered with the Franklin 6A-215-G8F engine of 215 hp. Republic expected to keep the Seabee's price below $10,000 if enough people bought it. Enough did not, so the Seabee went out of production in 1948.

Interestingly, the Seabee's configuration and target price resulted from a market survey of 10,000 licensed pilots to determine exactly what they wanted in the way of a personal airplane. So much for market surveys.

While the Seabee was not produced in great numbers, it remains the only low-cost (relatively speaking) amphibian available in today's used plane market.

Republic Seabee, Model RC-3 (1948)

Wing span	37 ft, 8 in	Cruising speed	100 mph (87 kt)
Empty weight	1,950 lb	Stalling speed	58 mph (51 kt)
Gross weight	3,000 lb	Initial climb	700 ft/min
Useful load	1,050 lb	Service ceiling	12,000 ft
Maximum speed	120 mph (104 kt)	Range (75 gal)	560 sm

Rockwell Commander 112A and 114

The Rockwell Commander 112 was introduced in 1972, powered with the IO-360-C1DC Lycoming, rated at 200 hp at 2,700 rpm. About 150 were built before the factory recalled them to correct poor cabin ventilation, air leaks, and other problems, mostly attributable to sloppy production techniques. This, plus the fact that the early seventies were bad years for all general aviation manufacturers, certainly contributed to the slow acceptance of this

The 1948 Republic SeaBee is the only low-cost amphibian available in the used plane market.

new design in the marketplace. Fewer than 250 Rockwell 112s were sold during its first three years of production. Not until late 1975 did sales of the debugged craft—now designated the Rockwell 112A—reach impressive levels.

The 112A, now built by experienced aircraftsmen under an effective quality-control program, is directly competitive with the Cherokee Arrow, Cardinal RG, and Beech Sierra. It is a mite slower than the competition, but it has good features of its own: good looks, a wide (if short) cabin, excellent landing characteristics, and the fact that it is one of the few light aircraft currently offered that is designed to withstand vertical gust loads of 50 ft/sec (now required by FAR Part 23.7).

This safety guarantee appears to have imposed no weight penalty on the 112A, because while it is close to the Arrow, Cardinal RG, and Sierra 200 in exterior dimensions, it has an empty weight below both the Sierra and Cardinal RG. Further, its gross weight (and useful load) is clearly dictated solely by power considerations, because the 260-hp Rockwell 114 uses the same airframe and is certified at a 400-lb greater gross weight.

The Rockwell 114 appeared in 1976, and as mentioned above, it is a 112A with a more powerful engine, the Lycoming IO-540-T4A5D of 260 hp. The additional power makes a significant difference. The cost of that difference is $9,000 on the new airplanes. In addition to nearly 400 lb more useful load, this also buys another 20 mph of cruising speed, more fuel capacity, and, in fact, more of just about everything in the way of performance.

These airplanes have good flying habits, and there are few Rockwell Commander owners who will not mention how nice they are to land. Their trailing-beam gear legs, first proven on the Ercoupes, are largely responsible for that.

Landing-gear and flap-limit speeds are 149 mph (130 kt) and 172 mph (150 kt), respectively, which allows rapid descents without overcooling the engine.

There are a lot of nice touches in the Rockwell Commander's "human environment" that make it a comfortable and fatigue-free craft to fly. All systems controls are handy to the pilot's right hand; there is a single master switch for all avionics; and since the flaps are wired into the gear-up warning circuit, an audible warning sounds if the flaps are extended beyond 25° with the wheels up.

Rockwell Commander 112A and 114

	112A **(200 hp, 1974)**	**114** **(260 hp, 1976)**
Wing span	32 ft, 9 in	32 ft, 9 in
Length	24 ft, 10 in	25 ft
Height	8 ft, 5 in	8 ft, 5 in
Empty weight	1,688 lb	1,790 lb
Gross weight	2,650 lb	3,140 lb
Useful load	962 lb	1,350 lb
Wing loading	17.4 lb/sq ft	20.7 lb/sq ft
Power loading	13.3 lb/hp	12.1 lb/hp
Baggage capacity	200 lb	200 lb
Maximum speed	171 mph (149 kt)	——
Cruising speed	161 mph (140 kt)	180 mph (152 kt)
Stalling speed	62 mph (53 kt)	63 mph (54 kt)
Initial climb	1,020 ft/min	1,054 ft/min
Service ceiling	13,900 ft	16,800 ft
Range	600 sm (48 gal)	

The Rockwell Commander 112A is another entry in the fuel-conscious 200-hp retractable class.

6

Used Single-Engine Turbocharged Airplanes

Single-engine turbocharged airplanes are not for everyone. In fact, they are not for the majority of pilots. Efficient high-altitude, high-speed cruising depends upon favorable winds and trip lengths of more than 300 miles. It also demands an instrument rating for all practical purposes, an oxygen system, and a greater investment in your flying machine.

The fact that the boom in single-engine turbocharged airplanes did not develop as expected when they were introduced back in 1966 was surely in part the result of the above-listed limitations. It was also owed, I suspect, to a deficient "comfort factor." The nose-bag oxygen mask is an uncomfortable anachronism.

There are, of course, some commercial pilots and a relative few private pilots who make good use of a single-engine turbocharged aircraft, airmen (airpersons?) who regularly haul heavy loads out of—and over—mountainous terrain, for example.

But do not expect a turbocharger to work miracles in getting you out of a mountain airport on a hot day. True, it will pack the air through your intake manifold, and that will help a lot; but it cannot supercharge the air mass that your propeller is working in or that your wings must use for support.

Aircraft cabin pressurization—and the shirtsleeve environment that it allows—is the key to practical, everyday high-altitude flight, at least for any so-called mass market. And at this writing, the pressurized Cessna Centurion, introduced in 1978, is the only single-engine airplane manufactured with this feature. Priced at $107,330 (fully equipped with avionics), it is obviously not for the mass market. Mooney's Mustang proved itself a failure, the only other attempt at it.

Here are the single-engine turbocharged airplanes available in the used market:

Beechcraft Turbo Bonanza, V35 series, 1966–71.
Bellanca Turbo Viking 300, 1969–present.
Cessna Turbo Super Skylane, TP206 series, 1966–71.
Cessna 206 Turbo Skywagon, TU206 series, 1966–72.
Cessna Turbo Stationair, 1972–present.
Cessna Turbo Centurion, 210 series, 1966–present.
Cessna Pressurized Centurion, introduced in 1978.
Lake Turbo Buccaneer, 1972–present.
Mooney Mk 22 Mustang, 1969.
Piper Turbo Comanche, PA-24-260TC, 1966–71.
Rockwell 112TC-A Commander, 1974–present.
Piper Turbo Arrow III, introduced in 1977.

Bolt-on turbo superchargers, produced by the Rajay Corporation, are available for other single-engine craft, including the Model 33 Debonair/Bonanza, most Mooneys, the Piper Cherokee Six, and the Cessna 180. Uninstalled cost currently averages $6,500 per unit.

The 1969 Beechcraft Turbo Bonanza V35A-TC.

The 1971 Cessna Turbo Centurion II.

The 1978 Cessna pressurized Centurion.

The 1969 Cessna Turbo Skywagon 206.

Controls of the 1978 pressurized Centurion.

	Beechcraft Bonanza V35B-TC	Bellanca Turbo Viking 300
Cruising speed	230 mph (200 kt)	235 mph (204 kt)
Climb rate	1,225 ft/min	1,800 ft/min
Gross weight	3,400 lb	3,325 lb
Empty weight	1,035 lb	2,010 lb
Useful load	1,365 lb	1,315 lb
Range	1,080 sm (80 gal)	1,379 sm (92 gal)

	Cessna Turbo Skywagon 206	Cessna Turbo Stationair
Cruising speed	184 mph (160 kt)	184 mph (160 kt)
Climb rate	1,030 ft/min	1,030 ft/min
Gross weight	3,600 lb	3,600 lb
Empty weight	1,810 lb	1,935 lb
Useful load	1,790 lb	1,665 lb
Range (80 gal)	770 sm	761 sm

	Cessna Turbo 207 Skywagon	Piper Turbo Comanche
Cruising speed	176 mph (153 kt)	228 mph (199 kt)
Climb rate	885 ft/min	1,320 ft/min
Gross weight	3,800 lb	3,200 lb
Empty weight	1,980 lb	1,894 lb
Useful load	1,820 lb	1,306 lb
Range	726 sm (80 gal)	1,180 sm (86 gal)

	Cessna Turbo Centurion	Cessna Pressurized Centurion
Cruising speed	225 mph (196 kt)	227 mph (198 kt)
Climb rate	1,030 ft/min	930 ft/min
Gross weight	3,800 lb	4,000 lb
Empty weight	2,240 lb	2,345 lb
Useful load	1,576 lb	1,671 lb
Range (90 gal)	950 sm	930 sm

	Lake Turbo Buccaneer	Rockwell Commander 112TC-A
Cruising speed	171 mph (149 kt)	181 mph (157 kt)
Climb rate	800 ft/min	1,023 ft/min
Gross weight	2,400 lb	2,850 lb
Empty weight	1,575 lb	1,750 lb
Useful load	825 lb	1,100 lb
Range	530 sm (40 gal)	1,015 sm (68 gal)

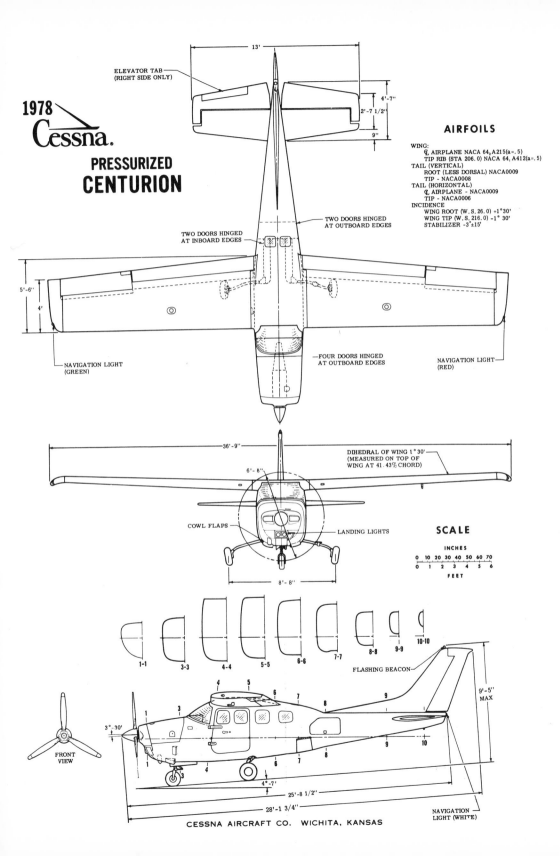

1978 Cessna.

PRESSURIZED CENTURION

13'

ELEVATOR TAB
(RIGHT SIDE ONLY)

4'-7"
2'-7 1/2"
9"

AIRFOILS

WING:
  ℄ AIRPLANE NACA 64₁A215(a=.5)
  TIP RIB (STA 206.0) NACA 64₁A412(a=.5)
TAIL (VERTICAL)
  ROOT (LESS DORSAL) NACA0009
  TIP - NACA0008
TAIL (HORIZONTAL)
  ℄ AIRPLANE - NACA0009
  TIP - NACA0006
INCIDENCE
  WING ROOT (W.S.26.0) +1°30'
  WING TIP (W.S.216.0) -1°30'
  STABILIZER -3°±15'

TWO DOORS HINGED
AT OUTBOARD EDGES

TWO DOORS HINGED
AT INBOARD EDGES

5'-6"
4'

NAVIGATION LIGHT
(GREEN)

FOUR DOORS HINGED
AT OUTBOARD EDGES

NAVIGATION LIGHT
(RED)

36'-9"

6'-8"

DIHEDRAL OF WING 1°30'
(MEASURED ON TOP OF
WING AT 41.43% CHORD)

COWL FLAPS

LANDING LIGHTS

SCALE

INCHES
0 10 20 30 40 50 60 70
0 1 2 3 4 5 6
FEET

8'-8"

1-1   3-3   4-4   5-5   6-6   7-7   8-8   9-9   10-10

FLASHING BEACON

9'-5"
MAX

3°-30'

FRONT
VIEW

4'-7'

25'-8 1/2"

28'-1 3/4"

NAVIGATION
LIGHT (WHITE)

CESSNA AIRCRAFT CO.   WICHITA, KANSAS

7
Used Reciprocating Twin-Engine Airplanes

When a pilot moves up to twins, the reasons have to be well justified unless the object is simply to spend money. Twins are more complex, harder to fly and manage, can be more dangerous if an engine is lost—but provide some excellent benefits to the prospective buyer seeking speed, payload, and safety benefits.

The FAA is projecting an increase in both multiengine aircraft and in pilots up through the mid-1980s. The major aircraft manufacturers have also not only introduced successive improvements in their twin-engine aircraft but have brought back the true light twin into the marketplace. Beech, Cessna, Piper, and Gulfstream-American (formerly Grumman-American) are manufacturing a new breed of multi whose stall speed and V_{mc} are within a few knots of each other, virtually eliminating minimum single-engine control-speed worries (unless one is foolish enough to stall a twin near the ground).

The improved safety factor is single-engine reliability at night and in IFR conditions, assuming the considered twin will actually fly and maintain level flight on one engine. Multis under 6,000 lb gross weight are not required to maintain level flight at gross weight on one engine, so having two fans out there is no guarantee of sailing along undisturbed when one quits. Ambient conditions and a host of other factors determine just what a twin will do on one engine, and as often as not all you get is an extended glide.

But twins offer comfort, speed, and room if you need it. Just make sure you look carefully, since twins are more headache to maintain and keep proficient in.

Rockwell Aero Commander 500 Series (1951–78)

Without doubt, Ted Smith's Commanders have been in the market longer than all other twins, and they are still being built in different forms. The 500 series survives as the Rockwell Shrike, with a lineage going back to the Douglas A-20.

The prototype Aero Commander flew on April 27, 1948, and the first Model 520 came out of the Bethany, Oklahoma, plant in August 1951, with two 260-hp Lycomings and six seats. By 1955, the 520 and 560 led the industry in sales. Since that time, despite corporate problems, the Aero Commander has been one of the most available of all twins.

These aircraft pioneered the day of the general aviation twin with longitudinal and directional electric trim, electric fuel shutoff valves, constant-speed full-feathering three-bladed props, supercharging, and pressurization.

In recent years, since a peak production run of fifty airplanes in 1974, the Shrike has been produced in fewer numbers. The Cessna 310 will cruise faster, fly farther, carry a bigger load, and perform better on one engine. But there is a special feel to the Commander, since it is bigger than most light twins. In turbulence there is good directional control because of the big vertical fin. The ample wing area and high aspect ratio give the aircraft a low stalling speed and docile handling characteristics. It is very easy to land, and the forward visibility is outstanding, especially in turns.

On takeoff the airplane will stick to the runway until you pull it off, which means a ground run past V_{mc} and best single-engine climb speed—a very comforting feeling. But if short fields have to be negotiated, the Commander can get off rather quickly.

Passenger comfort is very good, especially in turbulence, and exit and entry are made with ease. If one is going to fly people in comfort for a relatively low cost, reason points to checking out a Commander.

Though performance is not blistering when comparing charts with other twins, the Commander is a solid, reliable bird: no pitch changes with flaps and gear down—and touchdowns can be very soft with little experience. The airplane does not demand a great deal from the pilot overall, and this has to be an important factor for the prospective pilot who is not going to fly it every day.

As with all twins being considered, payload, range, and fuel have to be traded off to some extent. On the earlier Commanders this is especially true. Make sure to run several weight and balance problems on any 500-series aircraft you intend to buy, to be sure it will do what you require, from the first 520s to the newest plush Shrike Esquire IIs.

1951 Aero Commander 520

Engines: Lycoming GO-435A, 260 hp
Gross weight: 4,800 lb

PERFORMANCE
Stall speed: No flaps, 69 mph (60 kt)
                    Full flaps, 61 mph (53 kt)
Service ceiling at rated power:
    Two engines, 23,000 ft
    One engine, 8,500 ft
Cruising speed at 75% power, sea level:
    184 mph (160 kt)
Cruising speed at 10,000 ft, 70% power:
    194 mph (169 kt)
Rate of climb at sea level: 1,650 ft/min
Maximum range, 105 gal: 800 mi

The six-place Aero Commander 520 entered production in 1951.

1978 Spanair Shrike Esquire II

Engines: Lycoming IO-540-E1B5, 290 hp

Propellers: 3-blade, constant-speed, 80-in diameter

TBO: 1,400 h

Seats: 6

PERFORMANCE

Maximum rate of climb: 1,350 ft/min

Single-engine rate of climb: 266 ft/min

Single-engine climb gradient at 93 kt (Vy): 171 ft/nm

Service ceiling: 19,400 ft

Single-engine service ceiling: 6,500 ft

Maximum speed: 215 mph (187 kt)

Maximum cruise at 9,000 ft, 75% power: 203 mph (176 kt)

Duration at maximum cruise: 4.8 h

Stalling speed, clean: 73 mph (68 kt)

Stalling speed, full flaps: 67 mph (59 kt)

WEIGHTS

Empty weight: 5,136 lb

Useful load: 1,614 lb

Payload with full fuel: 628 lb

Gross weight: 6,750 lb

WING AREAS AND LOADING

Wing area: 255 sq ft

Wing loading: 26.47 lb/sq ft

Power loading: 11.63 lb/hp

DIMENSIONS

Length: 36 ft, 10 in

Height: 14 ft, 6 in

Wing span: 49 ft, 6 in

FUEL

Usable fuel capacity: 156 gal (936 lb)

The Grand Commander appeared in 1965. This 240-mph craft was also offered with pressurization.

Aerostar 600 Series (1967–78)

Another Ted Smith design, the Piper Aerostar has been the "hot ship" of the twin-engine market. Smith's desire, after his successful Aero and Jet Commander, was to design an aerodynamically clean airframe with interchangeable parts and covered with thick flush-riveted skin to bear most of the stress. This meant minimal internal structure, a subsequent reduction in weight, and a large boost in performance. The cabin was placed entirely ahead of the wing spar, making it difficult to overload with a wide CG (center of gravity) range.

In November 1966 the prototype flew. The first production version had 290-hp Lycomings to give it a cruise of 250 mph at 70 percent power at 10,000 ft and gross weight. Corporate ownership changes and machinations kept production rates low until the mid-seventies, but this fast twin found a ready market. The machine even holds the world's speed record for 500-km and 1,000-km closed courses—305 mph.

The speed, range, short-field capability, and excellent single-engine maneuvering of the Aerostar make it a very desirable piece of equipment. It will carry full IFR equipment, full fuel, and four people with baggage and not exceed gross weight. As a matter of fact, at any legal loading it is impossible to get outside the CG envelope.

With a wing span shorter than many singles, the machine's wing loading is high—32.4 lb/sq ft—which means fast climbs and approaches and the "hot" reputation. Regardless, any competent pilot can handle an Aerostar, because it is designed with the pilot in mind. Workloads are light enough to permit the pilot to stay "ahead" of the aircraft's speed. Single-engine routines are easy because of the logical arrangement of engine switches and levers. Visibility is excellent. And what a joy preflight is when all three fuel drain points are at one point on the lower fuselage.

Some have criticized the cabin volume, claiming passengers are cramped, but one has to trade something for such performance. A shorter flight a bit cramped can be a plus when the seats are comfortable and the windows so large as to ease the feeling of being hemmed in. But there are competing aircraft that offer greater comfort and convenience with sacrifices in efficiency or performance.

Some of the Piper Aerostar's problems center around the noise level near the props, and the delicate systems. The prop tips pass close to the skin, and at high rpm, noise can be intense. The hydraulics are a bit finicky, and standby electric pumps were installed on some as an option to give some security to the one on the right engine. If you want this security, ask if one is installed. The system is always pressurized, which means it is prone to seepage. The jewellike quality of such a clean design means that all gear doors must fit and sequence properly. Get a mechanic who knows the airplane if you want best results.

1975 Piper Aerostar 600

Engines: Lycoming IO-540, normally aspirated: 290 hp at 2,575 rpm

PERFORMANCE
Maximum speed at sea level: 260 mph (226 kt)
Cruising speed
  70% at 10,000 ft: 250 mph (217 kt)
  55% at 10,000 ft: 223 mph (194 kt)
Stalling speed (dirty, power off): 77 mph (67 kt)
Rate of climb
  At sea level: 1,850 ft/min
  Single engine: 450 ft/min
  Service ceiling: 22,000 ft
  Single engine service ceiling: 6,300 ft

Designer Ted Smith's Aerostar series, with 290-hp engines, are the only midwing twins produced.

Takeoff distance: 1,095 ft
 Over 50-ft-obstacle: 2,120 ft
Landing distance: 932 ft
 Over 50-ft obstacle: 2,032 ft
Fuel capacity (usable): 170 gal
Range (maximum fuel, 45-min reserve):
 Maximum cruise, 250 mph: 1,063 mi
 Maximum range, 204 mph: 1,650 mi

SPEED LIMITATIONS (IAS)
Minimum control speed: 97 mph (84 kt)
Best rate-of-climb speed: 145 mph (135 kt)
 Single engine: 135 mph (117 kt)
Best angle-of-climb speed: 125 mph (109 kt)
 Single engine: 125 mph (109 kt)
Never-exceed speed: 278 mph (242 kt)
Maneuvering speed: 187 mph (158 kt)
Maximum flap-extension speed:
 20°, 180 mph (157 kt)
 Full flaps, 148 mph (129 kt)
Maximum gear-extension speed: 180 mph (157 kt)
Maximum gear-retraction speed: 150 mph (130 kt)

WEIGHTS
Gross weight: 5,500 lb
Maximum zero-fuel weight: 4,450 lb
Standard empty weight: 3,800 lb
Standard useful load: 1,700 lb
Maximum cabin load with full fuel: 629 lb

WING AREAS AND LOADING
Wing area: 170 sq ft
Wing loading: 32.3 lb/sq ft
Power loading: 9.5 lb/sq ft
Baggage capacity: 30 cu ft, 200 lb

DIMENSIONS
Wing span: 34 ft, 2.5 in
Length: 34 ft, 9.75 in
Height: 12 ft, 1.5 in

FUEL
Fuel consumption (maximum cruise): 34 gal/h
Usable fuel: 174.5 gal

Beechcraft Model 18 (1937–69)

The venerable Twin Beech has to be the DC-3 of general aviation—seemingly around since the beginning of it all and still going strong. From first flight on January 15, 1937, to the final Super H18 roll-out on November 26, 1969, the Model 18 increased in gross weight by 3,200 lb with a 40-mph boost in cruising speed. It was adaptable, to say the least. The first examples cruised at 196 mph for 1,000 mi, weighing 6,700 lb gross.

During World War II the 18 produced more than 5,000 trained pilots, gunners, bombardiers, and navigators and served as utility transport. In early 1954, the Super 18 (Model E18S) came out with greater cabin area through an increase in fuselage height. By 1962 tricycle gear came as a factory-installed option. In all, 32 variations came out of the 8,088 built.

Six to ten people can fit into the 18s very comfortably as those wonderful P&W 450s pull it through the air—but they are thirsty engines for the speed. Other engines can be found on 18s, but R-985s are the standard power plants. Everything about the airplane harks back to another day—and most are tail-wheel airplanes known for their trickiness to land. Pilots say it takes more to land an 18 than a DC-3.

The flight deck is mostly metal—no plastic here. And the mixture of old and new abounds when one sees where some of the newer avionics are crammed. Levers pop out all over the place—oil shutters, oil cooler bypasses, oil shutoffs, cowl flaps—signifying those are radials out there. Preflight always requires pulling props through if one is not to stress the

The first Beech Model 18 made its maiden flight in January 1937.

bottom cylinders because of collected oil. Overall everything is massive, sturdy, big in feel and room.

The engines have a sound all their own as they grumble, bark, rasp, and thump. The airplane is very stable. In cruise one needs only to hold the wheel lightly. But it is heavy on the controls for maneuvering, as befits a heavy airplane—almost an airliner feel. Landing gear can be dropped at 160 and flaps at 120. The flight manual says, "Cross the end of the runway at approximately 95 mph and when about 15 feet off the ground, flare out slowly, touching down in a three-point attitude at approximately 80 mph." Then the fun starts. As with any conventionally geared airplane, the 18 does not stop flying until shut down and chocked.

The major problem on the airplane concerns the spars. An airworthiness directive requires an X ray of the wing's major load-bearing components every 1,550 h of flying time. They are getting old, and they can carry a great deal. Mechanics have also been known to misread spar X rays, and when the spar fails, the airplane has been blamed. As long as an X ray is done properly, the 18 is more than safe. But it is having a harder time making profits for people, and the day will come when it will be grounded for good.

1959 Beechcraft Model E18S

POWER
Engines: Two Pratt & Whitney R-985, 450 hp at 2,300 rpm
Propellers: Hamilton standard, 95-in diameter
Power loading: 10.77 lb/hp
Oil capacity: 7 gal per engine
TBO: 1,600 h

SPECIFICATIONS
Wing span: 49 ft, 8 in
Wing area: 310 sq ft
Wing loading: 31.2 lb/sq ft
Length: 35 ft, 2.5 in
Height: 10 ft, 5 in
Seats: 5 passengers, 2 crewmen
Baggage area: 36 cu ft (approx.)
Licensed category: Normal

The Beech Super 18 of 1954. Production of the "Twin Beech" finally ended in November 1969.

Gross takeoff weight, normal category: 9,700 lb

Gross landing weight: 9,400 lb

Empty weight: 5,910 lb

Fuel capacity, standard tanks: 198 gal

Fuel capacity with auxiliary tanks: 318 gal

PERFORMANCE

Maximum cruise speed: 214 mph (187 kt)

Maneuvering speed: 153 mph (133 kt)

Stall speed, clean: 93 mph (82 kt)

Stall speed, gear and full flaps: 84 mph (73 kt)

V_{mc}: 94 mph (83 kt)

Takeoff distance: 1,445 ft

Landing distance: 1,036 ft

Takeoff, over 50-ft obstacle: 1,980 ft

Landing, over 50-ft obstacle: 1,850 ft

Best rate of climb at sea level: 1,410 ft/min

Single-engine rate of climb: 255 ft/min

Service ceiling: 21,000 ft

Single-engine service ceiling: 7,750 ft

Maximum endurance range at 155 mph, standard tanks, no reserve: 4.2 h, 651 sm, no wind

Maximum range, auxiliary tanks, no reserve: 6.7 h, 1,038.5 sm, no wind

Average fuel consumption, normal cruise: 47.5 gal/h

SYSTEM OPERATIONS

Trim: Manual, elevator, rudder, aileron

Auxiliary fuel pump: Yes

Cowl flaps: Yes

Gear operation: Electric

Flaps: Electric

The Beechcraft Model 50 Twin Bonanza is a whopper of a light twin but is a pussycat to handle.

Beechcraft Model 50 Twin Bonanza (1951–63)

The Twin Bonanza was originally to be a huge Bonanza with two engines in the nose driving a single propeller. This was dropped in favor of adding an additional center section to the Bonanza fuselage mounted on a wing center section that supported two nacelles with Bonanza wings attached to their outer sides. The result was one whopper of an airplane in which the copilot sat in the center of a three-abreast bench seat!

As the 1950s went, the Model 50 proved to be a bit larger than what most people needed, although it remains a very useful aircraft with full tanks—it can still carry a load 900–1,300 mi at 190–225 mph at 65 percent power. And that wide cabin is very roomy for the four to five passengers. Such refinements as oxygen and an airstair door with fold-away steps came on the later models. There is plenty of room for avionics, and most T-bones can be seen with deicing equipment.

The airplane is one of the most docile for its size, and the big landing gear makes gentle landings a regular occurrence. Although it is not as fast as some of its younger brothers, the Model 50 provides a very smooth ride for all concerned.

The twelve-year production run produced 974 aircraft before the Model 65 Queen Air was evolved from the 50. The Travel Air and Baron filled the gap for smaller twins in the Beech line.

1962 Beechcraft Model J50 Twin Bonanza

Engines: Two Lycoming IGSO-480-A-IB6 supercharged, fuel-injected, 340 hp at 3,400 rpm

PERFORMANCE
(Maximum gross weight 7,300 lb at takeoff)
Cruising speed:
  70% power at 15,200 ft, 223 mph (194 kt)
  70% power at 10,000 ft, 213 mph (185 kt)
  65% power at 10,000 ft, 207 mph (180 kt)
High speed at 12,000 ft: 235 mph (204 kt)
Stall speed, gear and flaps down: 82.5 mph (72 kt)
Stall speed, gear and flaps up: 90 mph (78 kt)
Rate of climb at sea level:
  Two engines at 7,300 lb gross weight, 1,270 ft/min
  One engine at 7,300 lb gross weight, 195 ft/min
  One engine at 6,500 lb gross weight, 365 ft/min
Service ceiling:
  Two engines at 7,000 lb gross weight, 29,150 ft
  One engine at 6,500 lb gross weight (50 ft/min reserve), 15,200 ft
Maximum range (without allowance for fuel used during warm-up, taxi, take-off, and climb to altitude; no reserve):
  65% power at 10,000 ft (180 gal), 1,095 mi
  65% power at 10,000 ft (230 gal), 1,400 mi

Endurance:
  65% power at 10,000 ft (180 gal), 5.3 h
  65% power at 10,000 ft (230 gal), 6.8 h
Takeoff distance (with 20° flaps):
  Ground run, 1,110 ft
  Total distance over 50-ft obstacle, 1,450 ft
Landing over 50-ft obstacle (full flaps, 7,000 lb):
  Ground run, 1,000 ft
  Total over 50-ft obstacle, 1,840 ft

WEIGHTS
Gross weight: 7,300 lb
Empty weight, dry: 4,460 lb
Useful load: 2,840 lb

WING AREAS AND LOADING
Wing area: 277.06 sq ft
Loading at gross weight: 26.4 lb/sq ft

BAGGAGE STORAGE AREAS
Forward compartment: 200 lb
Aft compartment: 200 lb

DIMENSIONS
Wing span: 45 ft, 11⅜ in
Length: 31 ft, 6.5 in
Height: 11 ft, 4 in
Cabin length: 119 in
Cabin width: 54 in
Cabin height: 51 in

FUEL AND OIL
Fuel standard inboard tanks: 88 gal
Fuel standard outboard tanks: 92 gal
Fuel auxiliary wing tanks: 50 gal
Oil (4 gal each): 8 gal

In the late 1950s Beech once again launched out into the blooming twin-engine market with their third two-fan aircraft, the Travel Air. The Model 95 was aimed at those who did not need an airplane as large as the Twin Bonanza or the Model 18 but who still wanted an extra engine.

Beechcraft Model 95 Travel Air (1958–68)

The aircraft turned out to be a very popular twin for the price. It later was supplanted by the Baron, but before it was all over, 719 of them came out of Wichita, and they remain very popular on the used market.

About as straightforward as they come, the Travel Air got an honest 200-mph 75 percent cruise out of her 180-hp Lycomings. Considering that the Baron gets 225 mph out of two 260-hp engines, the economy considerations are obvious. Though Beech quality is evident in such things as flush gas caps and workmanship, the 95 was aimed at keeping economy in the forefront. There is a landing light in the nose cone instead of radar and a realistic seating of four people, although seating for five was offered as an option. Without a great deal of avionics up front, the nose baggage compartment can hold 270 lb, making CG problems manageable. But that does not always mean a great deal when loading up a light twin. If you are looking at a 95 that has the optional extra fuel of 112 gal total, then around 800 lb is all that is left for you, passengers and baggage. For economy one often has to settle for limited range or load, but those figures are certainly generous even if four people are aboard.

Like all Beech products, the 95 is a very nice-flying airplane with solid yet responsive handling characteristics. Most Travel Air owners are very happy with what they have for the money, and the airplane deserves a close look if you are going to buy a light twin. The newer generation of Grumman, Beech, Piper, and Cessna light twins that began to come out in 1978 are the 95's closest competitors in performance—but look at the difference in price in the blue book (Appendix II). The 95 may be one of the most underrated used twins on the market.

The Beechcraft Model 95 Travel Air is one of the better buys in the used market, with a nice balance of economy and performance.

1967 Beechcraft Model E95 Travel Air

Engines: Lycoming IO-360-B1B, fuel-injected, 180 hp at 2,700 rpm

PERFORMANCE
Cruising speed
    75% power at 7,500 ft,
        200 mph (174 kt)
    65% power at 11,000 ft,
        195 mph (170 kt)
High speed, sea level: 210 mph (182 kt)
Range (includes warm-up, taxi, takeoff, and climb to altitude with a 45-min reserve at maximum range speed):
    65% power, 195 mph
        112 gal, 1,035 mi
    Maximum range, 50% power,
        112 gal, 1,170 mi
    Endurance, 7.54 h
Rate of climb at sea level:
    Two engines, 4,200 lb, 1,250 ft/min
    Two engines, 3,700 lb, 1,560 ft/min
    One engine, 4,200 lb, 205 ft/min
    One engine, 3,700 lb, 355 ft/min

Service ceiling:
  Two engines (100 ft/min), 4,200 lb, 18,100 ft
  One engine (50 ft/min), 4,200 lb, 4,400 ft
Stall speed, gear down, flaps 28°: 70 mph
Takeoff distance:
  Sea level, zero wind, standard temp., 1,000 ft
  Total distance over 50-ft obstacle, 1,280 ft
Landing distance:
  At sea level, zero wind, standard temp., 980 ft
  Total distance over 50-ft obstacle, 1,590 ft

WEIGHTS
Gross weight: 4,200 lb
Empty weight: 2,650 lb
Useful load: 1,550 lb

WING AREA AND LOADING
Wing area: 199.2 sq ft
Loading at gross weight: 21.1 lb/sq ft

DIMENSIONS
Wing span: 37 ft, 10 in
Length: 25 ft, 11 in
Height: 9 ft, 6 in
Cabin length: 8 ft, 6 in
Cabin width: 3 ft, 6 in
Cabin height: 4 ft, 2 in

FUEL AND OIL
Standard fuel (2 mains, 40 gal each): 80 gal
Auxiliary fuel (mains + two 31-gal tanks): 112 gal
Oil: 4 gal

The first Beechcraft Baron appeared in 1961, and by 1978 more than 4,500 had been built. Above is the E55 model.

The 1978 Beechcraft Model 58 Barons. *Top to bottom:* Turbo Baron 58TC, Baron 58, and the Baron 58P.

Without question the beautiful Baron has been one of the most popular twins on the market and certainly one of the most adaptable. By 1978 total production came to around 4,500 since the first Model 55 rolled out in Kansas.

The Baron's design philosophy was similar to the Travel Air's: Beech wanted a twin to fill the gap between the Model 50 or 65 and the high-performance singles. What resulted was the first true "Bonanza with two engines" and a 75-percent cruise speed of 225 mph. The family has now

Beechcraft Models 55 and 58 Baron (1961–78)

121

grown to the stretched Model 58, which can come turbocharged and pressurized to fly at high altitudes with ease.

Any Bonanza pilot will feel right at home with the Baron because of the same basic cabin structure, gear system, and controls. Passengers will like the well-appointed interior and the solid feel inherent in Beech products.

Overall, the Baron is not difficult to fly, being straight-forward in most respects except for Beech's long tradition of placing prop controls left, throttles center, mixtures right. The aircraft gets up and off quickly, drops or retracts its gear in 4.5 sec, and climbs fast and handles well on one engine. The 58's twin-engine climb of 1,694 ft/min is the best of the unboosted twins, as is its 382-ft/min single-engine rate of climb. There is also an alternator on each engine.

Control response is light, much like the Bonanza's, but with a solid feel behind it. And that standard aileron trim is nice. The rapid gear is also a very good speed brake, since it can be dropped at 175 KIAS along with 15° approach flaps. The stall is mild, and slow flight turns can be made well into the prestall buffet.

Even with the optional long-range tanks filled, it can carry over 1,000 lb of payload or five people and some baggage—and then go 4.5 h (with reserves) at around 200 mph for 900 mi. Not bad.

The stretched versions, with rear double doors and club seating with a table in the middle, make it the most comfortable of the non-cabin-class twins for passengers. This can be a definite advantage if carrying passengers in as much comfort for as little money as possible is one of your reasons for buying a twin. But make sure to check out noise levels, as some are a bit noisy for the amount of money being put out.

By 1978 five versions were being produced in Wichita with engines of 260–310 hp and an optional 1,242-nm range with 194 gal of fuel. The stretched 58 is 10 in. longer with a lengthened wheel base. Barons can suit all types of missions with differing capability, so look carefully at what you need.

1968 Beechcraft Model B55 Baron

Engines: Continental IO-470-L, fuel-injected, 260 hp at 2,625 rpm

PERFORMANCE

Cruising speed:
    75% power at 7,000 ft,
        225 mph (196 kt)
    65% power at 10,500 ft,
        220 mph (191 kt)
High speed at sea level:
    236 mph (206 kt)
Range (includes warm-up, taxi, takeoff, climb to altitude with 45-min reserve): 45% power, 10,000 ft, 142 gal, 1,225 mi

Rate of climb at sea level:
    Two engines, 5,100 lb, 1,670 ft/min
    One engine, 5,100 lb, 320 ft/min
    One engine, 4,000 lb, 740 ft/min
Service ceiling:
    Two engines (100 ft/min), 5,100 lb, 19,700 ft
    One engine (50 ft/min), 5,100 lb, 7,000 ft
Stall speed (zero thrust), gear down, 28° flaps: 78 mph (68 kt)

Takeoff distance (20° flaps): 910 ft
   Over 50-ft obstacle, 1,255 ft
Landing distance (28° flaps): 840 ft
   Over 50-ft obstacle, 1,370 ft

WEIGHTS
Gross weight: 5,100 lb
Empty weight: 3,075 lb
Useful load: 2,025 lb

WING AREA AND LOADING
Wing area: 199.2 sq ft
Wing loading, gross weight:
   25.6 lb/sq ft

BAGGAGE STORAGE AREA
Rear compartment: 400 lb

Front compartment: 300 lb
Optional extended rear: 120 lb

DIMENSIONS
Wing span: 37 ft, 10 in
Length: 27 ft, 3 in
Height: 9 ft, 7 in
Cabin length: 8 ft, 6 in
Cabin width: 3 ft, 6 in
Cabin height: 4 ft, 2 in

FUEL AND OIL
Standard (2 mains, 2 auxiliary): 112 gal
Optional (2 mains, 2 auxiliary): 142 gal
Oil: 6 gal

1975 Beechcraft Model 58 Baron

Engines: Two Continental IO-520-C, 6-cylinder, fuel-injected, 285 hp at 2,700 rpm

PERFORMANCE
Maximum speed (sea level):
   242 mph (211 kt)
Cruise speed (75% at 7,000 ft):
   230 mph (200 kt)
Takeoff roll: 899 ft
Takeoff over 50-ft obstacle: 1,093 ft
Rate of climb: 1,694 ft/min
Rate of climb, single engine: 382 ft/min
Service ceiling: 17,800 ft
Service ceiling, single engine: 7,150 ft
Range (65%, takeoff, climb,
   45-min reserve): 1,220 sm
Stall speed (IAS, gear and flaps down):
   85 mph (74 kt)
Stall speed (IAS, gear and flaps up):
   96 mph (83 kt)

Landing roll: 1,044 ft
Landing over 50-ft obstacle: 1,469 ft

WEIGHTS
Gross weight: 5,400 lb
Standard empty: 3,215 lb
Standard useful load: 2,185 lb
Baggage capacity: 30 cu ft
Fuel capacity: 168 gal usable

DIMENSIONS
Wing span: 37 ft, 10 in
Length: 29 ft, 10 in
Height: 9 ft, 7 in
Wing area: 199.2 sq ft
Wing loading: 27.1 lb/sq ft
Cabin length: 9 ft, 4 in
Maximum cabin width: 3 ft, 6 in

The stately Queen Air was a direct outgrowth of the Twin Bonanza. If Beech was to develop a larger aircraft, then the Model 50 would certainly serve as a good airframe to build on. The prototype 65 flew on August 28, 1958, after experimental development with six Twin Bonanzas. (Incidentally, this aircraft is still flying in Germany.)

The "Queenie" has never been a very glamorous airplane, even with the later cosmetic change from slab to swept tail, but it is known for efficiency and reliability. In its years of manufacture, so far three major modifications

Beechcraft Model 65, 70, 80, and 88 Queen Air (1959–78)

123

have been adopted: the swept tail, cabin pressurization, and replacement of the Lycoming 480s with PT-6A turboprops. This last change introduced the wonderful Model 90 King Air, the leading turboprop in its class. The Model 99 airliner has also come from the noble Queen Air.

Although the aircraft is still being built (close to 1,000 so far), it has gone almost exclusively to the international market. It remains active on the used market because of its versatile interior. Configurations range from an open cabin to five commuter seats, to a full executive-style three-compartment interior. Seating ranges from seven to eleven. The bulkheads can be removed for cargo hauling, and cargo doors are options. And in a 14-ft cabin, one can have almost anything. One can get 18 ft in the B80, which can cruise at 196 kt with a 3,578-lb useful load for 1,300 nm. The Lycomings installed in the Queen Air are either 340 hp or 380 hp with supercharging.

The aircraft is another one of those honest-handling Beech airplanes. Though large by some standards, it is straight-forward, even docile, with very flattering landing gear in hard landings. In many ways it is the Twin Bonanza all over again, and it does have the solid feel one would expect from a mini-airliner. If you are going to need an airplane that can have a large load, this is the one. Just make sure you need something this big.

1966 Beechcraft Model 65 Queen Air

Engines: Lycoming IGSO-480-A1E6, fuel-injected, geared and super-charged with oil-cooled pistons, rated at 340 hp at 3,400 rpm

PERFORMANCE

Maximum takeoff weight: 7,700 lb
Maximum landing weight: 7,700 lb
Cruising speeds:
  70% power (2,750 rpm) at 10,000 ft, 205 mph (178 kt)
  65% power (2,600 rpm) at 10,000 ft, 200 mph (174 kt)
  45% power (2,500 rpm) at 10,000 ft, 166 mph (144 kt)
High speed at 12,000 ft: 239 mph (208 kt)
Cruise range (includes full allowance for fuel used during warm-up, taxi, take-off, and climb to altitude with a 45-min fuel reserve at maximum-range speed)

	180 gal	230 gal
70% power at 15,000 ft	695 mi	945 mi
70% power at 5,000 ft	705 mi	940 mi
65% power at 17,000 ft	775 mi	1,065 mi
65% power at 5,000 ft	800 mi	1,065 mi
65% power at 15,000 ft	1,000 mi	1,380 mi
65% power at 5,000 ft	1,060 mi	1,415 mi

Maximum endurance (no reserve):
| 35% power at 5,000 ft | 9.1 h | 11.8 h |

Fuel consumption:
  70% power, 42.3 gal/h
  65% power, 36.0 gal/h
  45% power, 22.7 gal/h
Rate of climb at sea level, two engines: 7,700 lb, 1,300 ft/min
Rate of climb at sea level, one engine, takeoff power:
  7,700 lb, 245 ft/min
  6,500 lb, 455 ft/min
Service ceiling, two engines (100 ft/ min) at 6,500 lb: 31,300 ft
Service ceiling, one engine (50 ft/min) at 6,500 lb: 15,500 ft
Stall speed (zero thrust):
  Gear and flaps down 30°, 80 mph (70 kt)

Gear and flaps up, 94 mph (82 kt)
Takeoff distance, 20° flaps:
   Ground run, 1,180 ft
   Total over 50-ft obstacle, 1,560 ft
Landing weight, 7,700 lb
Landing distance, 30° flaps:
   Ground run, 1,330 ft
   Total over 50-ft obstacle, 1,750 ft

WEIGHTS
Gross weight: 7,700 lb
Empty weight dry: 4,850 lb
Useful load (includes 36 lb
   of unusable fuel and oil): 2,850 lb
Available weight for passengers,
   baggage, and optional equipment
   with standard fuel tanks full: 1,674
   lb

WING AREA AND LOADING
Wing area: 277.06 sq ft
Wing loading at gross weight:
   27.8 lb/sq ft
Power loading at gross weight:
   12.03 lb/hp

BAGGAGE
Standard aft lavatory and baggage
   compartment: Capacity 350 lb

DIMENSIONS
Wing span: 45 ft, 10.5 in
Stabilizer span: 205.46 in
Length: 33 ft, 4 in
Height to top of fin: 14 ft, 2 in
Cockpit height: 57 in
Cockpit width: 52 in
Cabin length with standard aft lavatory
   installation: 214 in
Cabin width: 54 in
Cabin height: 57 in

FUEL AND OIL CAPACITY
Fuel capacity standard inboard tanks
   (44 gal each): 88 gal
Fuel capacity standard outboard tanks
   (46 gal each): 92 gal
Fuel capacity optional auxiliary
   wing tanks (25 gal each): 50 gal
Total: 230 gal (2.5 gal unusable)
Oil capacity (4 gal each):
   8 gal (2.9 gal unusable)

Versatile is the word for the unglamorous Beechcraft Queen Air series. This one is the Model 70.

The Beechcraft Model 88 Queen Air is powered with a pair of 380-hp engines and is pressurized.

The pressurized Beechcraft Duke B60 has a maximum cruise of 248 kt, and among cabin-class twins that tout comfort, the Duke has an edge.

125

The sleek Duke followed naturally as a gap filler between the Baron and the Queen Air in the Beech line of airplanes. Presently Duke represents the line between the P-Baron and the King Air—and the Duke holds its own here as one of the most popular twins with owner-pilots.

The wing is standard Beech in that the same airfoil serves the line from the Bonanza to the Super King Air, but the Duke will cruise tops at 248 kt on two 380-hp turbocharged engines, only 6 mph less than the Aerostar 601-P. Beech also broke its own tradition in that throttles, props, and mixture are in that order from the left seat.

The Duke is both a pilot pleaser and a passenger pleaser. Systems are simple and standard Beech—fuel is ON–OFF–CROSSFEED, flaps are indicated on the panel by three lights (red in transit, blue for 15° approach, amber for 30° full down), rapid gear extension. The cockpit is roomy with good visibility and the controls are like those in other Beech products—firm but responsive. The ailerons are quick, but the elevators are a bit heavy.

Passenger comfort is a primary consideration in the Duke: it is plush and quiet, with optional club seating for four. Cabin-class twins have always touted comfort, but the Duke has an edge. This feature is worth checking out if it is important to you in buying an airplane.

The Duke would normally fit into the chapter on turbocharged and pressurized versions of the twins being considered, but it is built with these features standard. At 25,000 ft the cabin stays at 10,000. The TBO on the Lycomings has risen from 800 h in 1968 to 1,600 h in 1978. Make sure to check these figures before buying one. In 1978 Beech also switched to a cheaper battery system, dropping the nickel-cadmium batteries.

Overall, the Duke is a Rolls Royce of an airplane that gets up there with the best of them—for a price. By the end of 1978, total production was approaching 500.

1969 Beechcraft Model A60 Duke

Engines: Two Lycoming TIO-541-E1A4, six-cylinder, turbocharged, fuel-injected, rated 380 hp at 2,900 rpm

PERFORMANCE

High speed at 23,000 ft: 286 mph (248 kt)

Cruising speeds:
- 75% power at 25,000 ft: 271 mph (235 kt)
- 75% power at 15,000 ft: 246 mph (214 kt)
- 65% power at 25,000 ft: 255 mph (255 kt)
- 65% power at 15,000 ft: 232 mph (201 kt)
- 45% power at 25,000 ft: 210 mph (182 kt)
- 45% power at 15,000 ft: 197 mph (171 kt)

Rate of climb at sea level, two engines:
- 6,725 lb, 1,615 ft/min
- 5,200 lb, 2,373 ft/min

Rate of climb at sea level, single engine:
- 6,725 lb, 319 ft/min
- 5,200 lb, 739 ft/min

Service ceiling:
- 6,725 lb, 31,300 ft

Service ceiling (single engine):
- 6,725 lb, 15,700 ft
- 5,200 lb, 23,800 ft

Pressurization: 4.6 differential

Aircraft altitude	Cabin altitude
10,500 ft	Sea level
21,200 ft	8,000 ft
24,700 ft	10,000 ft

Stall speed (at gross weight):
  Power off, flaps and gear down,
    87 mph (76 kt)
  Power off, flaps and gear up,
    98 mph (85 kt)
Takeoff distance (at gross weight):
  Ground run, 1,253 ft
  Total over 50-ft obstacle, 1,660 ft
Landing distance (at gross weight):
  Ground run, 1,590 ft
  Total over 50-ft obstacle, 2,340 ft
Range (includes warm-up, taxi, takeoff,
  climb to altitude, and 45-min reserve,
  reserve computed at 45% power; 204
  gal):
  75% power at 25,000 ft, 846 nm (973
    sm)
  75% power at 15,000 ft, 803 nm (924
    sm)
  65% power at 25,000 ft, 932 nm (1,073
    sm)
  65% power at 15,000 ft, 893 nm (1,027
    sm)
  45% power at 25,000 ft, 1,021 nm
    (1,175 sm)
  45% power at 15,000 ft, 1,009 nm
    (1,161 sm)

WEIGHTS
Gross weight: 6,725 lb
Empty weight (approx.): 4,100 lb
Useful load: 2,625 lb
Baggage compartment, rear: 315 lb
Baggage compartment, front: 500 lb

WING AREA AND LOADING
Wing area: 212.9 sq ft
Wing loading at gross weight:
  31.6 lb/sq ft

DIMENSIONS
Wing span: 39 ft, 3 in
Length: 33 ft, 10 in
Height: 12 ft, 4 in
Cabin length: 142 in
Cabin width: 50 in
Cabin height: 52 in
Passenger door: 47.5 in × 26.5 in
Baggage door: 23.5 in × 37.5 in

FUEL CAPACITY
Standard: 142 gal usable
Optional: 204 gal usable
Oil capacity (4 gal each engine):
  6.5 gal usable

In the 1950s and 1960s, when general aviation twins were coming into their own, the true light twin got left behind as the Travel Air and Apache went the way of all aluminum in favor of the Baron and Aztec. The light twin made an enormous comeback in 1978 with products (all very similar) from Beech, Gulfstream-American, Cessna, and Piper. The Model 76 was one of the three that made it out onto the market that year.

For all intents and purposes, the Duchess is a Sierra with two engines giving pilots the opportunity to choose between a top-of-the-line single or a relatively low-cost twin. With counterrotating propellers, the critical engine problem is solved, and V_{mc} is low enough to be less of a pucker factor than the larger twins. The 235 ft/min single-engine climb speed at sea level is healthier than most twins as well.

CG and weight problems are not very much of a factor at present, because of four-place seating and 600 lb of fuel. This leaves 870 lb out of the useful load for passengers and baggage. Fuel is managed by the simple ON–OFF–CROSSFEED system, and the landing gear is hydraulically operated by an electric pump (same one in the Sierra) so that it can cycle with an engine out.

**Beechcraft
Model 76
Duchess
(1978–   )**

127

The T-tail, the latest craze on the new light aircraft, is up above the prop wash, wing wake, and fuselage disturbances, which means less vibration. And the design has proven very effective in spin recovery, thanks to NASA flight tests for the past several years. There is less variation in trim, more effective pitch control, an extended CG and a new look for twin pilots (unless one has been flying a Super King Air, the daddy of the Beech T-tail).

The two 180-hp Lycoming engines pull four people and 180 lb of baggage at a maximum cruise of 166 kt for 780 nm. Naturally there are trade-offs in any twin, and one must consider whether an extra fan is worth the price to do a job a single can do more cheaply. But this new generation of twins will certainly introduce to multiengine flying many pilots who would not have tried it before. The bugs in the airplane remain to be discovered.

1978 Beechcraft Model 76 Duchess

Engines: Lycoming O-360, 180 hp each, with opposite-rotating propellers

PERFORMANCE

Maximum speed: 197 mph (171 kt)

Cruise speeds at average cruise weight of 3,600 lb:

Maximum cruise power (2,700 rpm) at 6,000 ft: 191 mph (166 kt)

Recommended cruise power (2,500 rpm) at 10,000 ft: 176 mph (153 kt)

Economy cruise power (2,300 rpm) at 12,000 ft: 172 mph (149 kt)

Cruise ranges at average cruise weight of 3,600 lb, with allowance for start, taxi, climb, descent, and 45-min reserve at economy cruise power:

Maximum cruise power at 6,000 ft, 623 nm (717 sm)

Recommended cruise power at 10,000 ft: 711 nm (818 sm)

Economy cruise power at 12,000 ft, 780 nm (898 sm)

Rate of climb at sea level:

Two engines, 1,248 ft/min

One engine, 235 ft/min

Service ceiling:

Two engines, 100 ft/min, 19,650 ft

One engine, 50 ft/min, 6,170 ft

Stall speeds:

Power off, flaps at 35°, 67 mph (58 kt)

Power off, flaps up, 78 mph (68 kt)

Takeoff distance:

Ground run, 1,017 ft

Total distance over 50-ft obstacle, 2,119 ft

Landing distance:

Ground run, 1,000 ft

Total distance over 50-ft obstacle, 1,880 ft

WEIGHTS

Maximum ramp weight: 3,916 lb

Maximum takeoff weight: 3,900 lb

Maximum landing weight: 3,900 lb

Empty weight: 2,446 lb

Useful load (standard airplane): 1,470 lb

DIMENSIONS

Wing span: 38 ft

Length: 29 ft

Height: 9 ft, 6 in

Wheel track: 10 ft, 7 in

Wheel base: 7 ft

FUEL CAPACITY

Usable fuel: 100 gal

The 1978 Beechcraft Model 76 Duchess is essentially a T-tailed Sierra with two engines, giving pilots a choice between a top-of-the-line single-engine or a relatively low-cost twin. Props are counterrotating.

The 1962 Cessna Skyknight seats five. Engines are TSIO-470-B Continentals of 260 hp each.

Cessna Models 310 and 320 (1954–78)

The good old 310 has long been the "hot ship" of postwar general aviation. Well over 5,000 have come out of Wichita into the eager hands of pilots who came to regard it as slippery, requiring above-average skill. And it was faster than most twins for some time.

Through the years, as befits a strong design, the 310 has retained its basic good looks with improved performance. Cosmetic changes have included bigger windows and one-piece windshields, but the airframe modifications have been of greater import—swept-back tail, canted tip tanks (for better spiral stability), new engine nacelles (replacing overwing exhausts with baggage lockers), ventral strake (improved lateral stability), new nose gear (better ground handling), a new cabin roof and rear window (for increased aft headroom), and a 400-series-style nose that lengthened the 310 by almost a yard.

129

When the long nose was added to the 310R in 1975, the 260-hp engines were dropped in favor of 285-hp Continentals, which powered the Turbo 310. This made it about as fast as the E55 Baron. Better handling characteristics resulted as well, and a better CG option with a 350-lb baggage and avionics bay out there.

In 1969 the 320 Skynight, a heavy-duty stretched 310, was replaced by the Turbo 310, and the later 340 took that place in the Cessna line. The 320 remains a fine performer for the money in used airplanes.

All 310s fly like airplanes are supposed to fly, and there is little question that the early models require some finesse to get them squeaked onto a runway. Stalls were shaky, violent things with plenty of warning, but spins were discussed as single-engine procedure. As the aircraft was steadily refined, these "hot" characteristics were slowly designed out, and by 1975 the 310 was being called docile and easy to land in spite of the high wing loading. Early 310s are noted for their heavy elevator forces, particularly at low air speeds and high angles of attack—they really hit the runway if flared too high. The R model seems to have solved that problem once and for all.

Regardless of the challenging characteristics of the earlier 310s, all of them are performers. With the proper check-out, any of them can suit one's needs, from personal transport with four seats to corporate use and six seats with plenty of baggage room. Just keep in mind that any twin has to compromise payload, range, and speed in varying proportions to do any job.

1972 Cessna Model 310Q

Engines: Two IO-470-VO 6-cylinder, fuel-injected, rated 260 hp at 2,625 rpm

Gross weight:	5,300 lb	4,500 lb
Speed (best power mixture):	236 mph (205 kt)	241 mph (209 kt)
Maximum speed at sea level		
75% power at 6,500 ft	221 mph (192 kt)	227 mph (198 kt)
Maximum recommended cruise,		
Range (normal lean mixture):		
Maximum recommended cruise		
75% power at 6,500 ft	774 mi	796 mi
600 lb usable fuel	3.55 h	3.55 h
No reserves	218 mph (190 kt)	224 mph (195 kt)
75% power at 6,500 ft	1,390 mi	1,428 mi
1,080 lb usable fuel	6.37 h	6.37 h
No reserves	218 mph	224 mph
Maximum range at 10,000 ft	1,729 mi	1,894 mi
1,080 lb usable fuel	9.44 h	10.77 h
No reserves	183 mph (159 kt)	176 mph (153 kt)
Rate of climb at sea level:		
Twin engine	1,495 ft/min	1,925 ft/min
Single engine	327 ft/min	463 ft/min
Service ceiling:		
Twin engine	19,500 ft	22,600 ft
Single engine	6,680 ft	9,930 ft

Gross weight: 5,300 lb   4,500 lb

	5,300 lb	4,500 lb
Gross weight:	5,300 lb	4,500 lb
Takeoff at sea level:		
Ground run		
Total distance over 50-ft obstacle	1,519 ft	1,026 ft
Landing at sea level:	1,795 ft	1,228 ft
Landing roll	582 ft	406 ft
Total distance over 50-ft obstacle	1,697 ft	1,521 ft

Empty weight (approx.): 3,223 lb
Baggage allowable: 600 lb
Wing loading: 29.6 lb/sq ft
Power loading: 10.2 lb/hp
Fuel capacity (total):
    Standard, 102 gal (612 lb)
    Optional, 143 gal (858 lb, wing auxiliary tanks)
    Optional, 184 gal (1,104 lb, wing auxiliaries plus wing locker transfer tanks)
Oil capacity (total): 6 gal
Wing span: 36 ft, 11 in
Wing area: 179 sq ft
Length: 29.25 ft
Height: 10.43 ft
Stall: 72 mph (63 kt)
V_{mc}: 86 mph (75 kt)

The 1964 Cessna 310 is a five/six-place craft with a maximum cruise of 194 kt, and a 6-h range with reserves.

The Turbo 310Q of 1974.

The 1976 Cessna 310. The Citation nose was added in 1975, along with the 285-hp engines that power the Turbo 310's.

131

Cessna Model 337 Skymaster (1963–78)

The Skymaster is one of the few genuine Cinderella stories in general aviation. Appearing as the fixed-gear Model 336, the aircraft died in less than a year, after being touted as a twin that single-engine pilots could fly with a minimum of additional ratings. The FAA did not buy the idea, and a new centerline thrust rating was created just for the Skymaster.

Cessna did not give up on their "mixmaster, push-pull" idea. With the addition of retractable gear, the Model 337 entered the market and has found wide acceptance ever since as a fast twin without a lot of worry for the busy pilot.

The earlier models have some differences worth noting. Find out if the one you are looking at has to be started front engine first (battery located forward of the front firewall). Accidents revealed that if one did not start the rear engine first, the forward engine drowned out the confirming noise from the back. Most Skymasters tend to be noisy, so check this feature in flight before you buy.

The Skymaster is basically a four- or five-place airplane; with six seats, baggage has to be carried in a pod underneath the fuselage. When the Pressurized Skymaster was introduced in 1972, the rear baggage door was eliminated and the Turbo Skymaster dropped (later reintroduced in 1978).

Fuel and electrical systems are simple, adding to pilot calm. Controls are firm but responsive, with straight-forward stalls. But the 337 is heavy, as befits an honest-to-goodness twin. On takeoff a placard reads, LEAD WITH REAR ENGINE POWER, CHECK RPM & FUEL FLOW. Pilots have taken off without realizing that the rear engine was dead. The props counterrotate, so there is no torque, no propeller effect, no V_{mc} to worry about. But if one is lost on takeoff, the best advice is to leave the gear alone until sufficient altitude, since all those doors popping out produce quite a bit of drag.

Before 1972 the rear engine was more efficient than the forward and the wing's angle of incidence was negative. A bigger front prop and change to positive incidence made takeoffs less a 707 haul-it-off affair.

By 1977 weather radar was offered as an option (a first for a nose-mounted-engine general aviation airplane). All in all, the 337 is one of the lowest-priced twins on the market, and it gets along at 170 kt at 75 percent power for 970 mi if a few people and some luggage are aboard. There is no way one can load it up and fly long distances. The combination of rugged

The 1964 Cessna Model 337 Skymaster with fixed landing gear. Maximum cruise is 152 kt; range is 3.5 h with reserves.

132

gear and low takeoff and landing speeds make it a good airplane for unimproved fields as well. Visibility is better than in most low-wing airplanes because the pilots are ahead of the leading edge. If you can find one with Robertson STOL conversion, it can really get in and out of tight spots.

A 337 flight is well worth your time if you are serious about buying a twin.

1970 Cessna Model 337 Super Skymaster

Engines: Two 6-cylinder, fuel-injection engines, rated 210 hp at 2,800 rpm

Gross weight: 4,440 lb*

Speed (best power mixture):
  Top speed at sea level, 199 mph (174 kt)
  Cruise, 75% power at 5,500 ft, 191 mph (166 kt)

Range (normal lean mixture):
  Cruise, 75% power at 5,500 ft, 760 mi 92 gal, no reserve, 4.0 h, 190 mph (165 kt)
  Cruise, 75% power at 5,500 ft, 1,060 mi 128 gal, no reserve, 5.6 h, 190 mph (165 kt)
  Optimum range at 10,000 ft, 1,354 mi 128 gal, no reserve, 9.3 h, 144 mph (125 kt)

Rate of climb at sea level:
  Twin engine, 1,180 ft/min
  Front engine only, 285 ft/min
  Rear engine only, 370 ft/min

Service ceiling:**
  Twin engine, 19,300 ft
  Front engine only, 6,500 ft
  Rear engine only, 8,500 ft

Takeoff:
  Ground run, 910 ft
  Total distance over 50-ft obstacle, 1,565 ft

Landing:
  Ground roll, 700 ft
  Total distance over 50-ft obstacle, 1,650 ft

Stall speed:
  Flaps up, power off, 78 mph (68 kt)
  Flaps down, power off, 69 mph (60 kt)

Empty weight (approx.): 2,660 lb

Useful load: 1,780 lb

Baggage allowable: 365 lb

Wing loading: 21.9 lb/sq ft

Power loading: 10.6 lb/hp

Fuel capacity:
  Total, standard, 93 gal
  Total, optional, 131 gal

Oil capacity (total): 5 gal

Wing span: 38 ft, 2 in

Wing area: 202.5 sq ft

Length: 29 ft, 9 in

Height (with depressed nose strut): 9 ft, 4 in

*Maximum takeoff weight is 4,440 lb. Maximum landing weight is 4,400 lb.
**Single-engine service ceiling increases 400 ft for each 30 min of flight.

The Cessna Skymaster eventually came into its own following a number of important changes, including retractable landing gear.

133

The pressurized Skymaster for 1978.

Cessna Model 340 (1972–78)

Cessna, after closing out its 320, did not waste much time in coming back with a better 300-series twin to replace the Skynight. The 340 is basically 310 wings, engines, and tail with a new fuselage. But the difference is marked. This airplane was aimed at the Duke market. It is a cabin-class six-seater, turbocharged, pressurized business machine in its own right rather than a modified version of something slower and lower.

Until newer 310-hp engines replaced the 285-hp Continentals in 1976, the 340 had underwhelming single-engine performance: it was built as a heavy, pressurized machine from the start but on Model 310 power and wings. With the 340A the problems were solved, though the older 340s do fine.

The pressurization system is very similar to that in the larger 414 and 421, and it is very simple to operate. Single-engine flying with big power changes does not produce any popping or surging. This reflects the Cessna philosophy of single-pilot operation in the 340 to attract 310, Baron, and Aztec owners. That Cessna was right has been proven by the subsequent addition of a pressurized Skymaster, Baron, and Aerostar to compete in this class of buyers.

The 340 is slower in cruise than the Baron or Aerostar, but its airport requirements are lower than the others because of its lower power and wing loading. Automatic turbo controllers add to the simplicity, and sound levels are fairly quiet. A nice Cessna option on 340s is the prop synchrophaser that can be adjusted not only to hold sync but to phase the propellers for the quietest angle. If quiet is on your list of requirements, check out a 340 with this feature.

Stalls and slow flight are very docile, and as stated before, the 1976 and later As have an extra 50 hp for better climb and single-engine work. And the 340 lands very easily, even more easily than its 310 predecessors.

Of the aircraft in its class, the 340 is generally the lowest priced, carrying more fuel with least airport requirements and the roomiest cabin. It is also the slowest. Again, check your requirements in buying a twin to see if they fit. The 340s are good contenders.

134

1972 Cessna 340

Engines: TSIO-520K, turbocharged, fuel-injected, 285 hp
Useful load: 2,278 lb
Gross weight: 5,975 lb
Speed (best power mixture):
  Maximum at sea level, 221 mph (192 kt)
  Maximum at 16,000 ft, 260 mph (226 kt)
  Maximum recommended cruise, 75% power at 10,000 ft, 219 mph (191 kt)
  Maximum recommended cruise, 75% power at 20,000 ft, 241 mph (210 kt)
Range (recommended lean mixture):
  Maximum recommended cruise
    75% power at 10,000 ft, 663 mi
    600 lb, 3.08 h
    No reserve, 215 mph (187 kt)
    75% power at 10,000 ft, 1,193 mi
    1,080 lb, 5.54 h
    No reserve, 215 mph (187 kt)
    75% power at 20,000 ft, 726 mi
    600 lb, 3.08 h
    No reserve, 236 mph (205 kt)
    75% power at 20,000 ft, 1,306 mi
    1,080 lb, 5.54 h
    No reserve, 236 mph (205 kt)
    Maximum range at 20,000 ft, 1,432 mi
    1,080 lb, 7.11 h
    No reserve, 202 mph (175 kt)

Rate of climb at sea level:
  Twin engine, 1,500 ft/min
  Single engine, 250 ft/min
Service ceiling:
  Twin engine, 26,500 ft
  Single engine, 12,100 ft
Takeoff performance:
  Ground run, 1,760 ft
  Total distance over 50-ft obstacle, 2,430 ft
Landing performance:
  Landing roll, 765 ft
  Total distance over 50-ft obstacle, 1,840 ft
Empty weight (approx.): 3,697 lb
Baggage allowable: 930 lb
Wing loading: 32.47 lb/sq ft
Power loading: 10.48 lb/hp
Fuel capacity (total):
  Standard, 102 gal
  Optional, 143 gal
  Standard, optional, and wing lockers, 184 gal
Wing span: 38 ft, 1 in
Length of airplane: 34 ft, 4 in

The pressurized Cessna 340 is the follow-up to the discontinued Skyknight. Pictured is a 1973 model.

In 1965 Cessna introduced the Model 411 into a relatively uncluttered market area—the unpressurized, turbocharged big twin for cargo hauling or office space aloft. Then came the 401 and 402 and finally the 404, along with enough different names to confuse anyone. But the idea was the same.

By 1972 the 401 and 402 became known as the Utiliner and the Businessliner (not respectively—there was the 401 and 402 Utiliner, etc., if that makes sense). The Utiliner was a commuter or cargo hauler with wide double doors, lots of baggage space, room for ten people, and instant convertality from passenger to cargo configuration. The 401 was the smaller of the two. The Businessliner had standard seating for six to eight, with all kinds of office goodies like fold-out desks, a toilet, and so on. The 300-hp engines did a fine job in hauling 2,500 lb of fuel and payload at 218 mph and 75 percent power.

As if these options were not enough, Cessna built the 404 Titan (page 138) to enter the business, commuter, air taxi, and cargo markets. The dual option package was offered once again—the Courier for high-density seating and cargo, the Ambassador for airborne office space. What the 404 had that made it different was 375-hp engines and a new wing without tip tanks. Useful load was boosted to 3,600 lb with a 65 percent cruise of 207 mph. The airplane is a midway point between the 402 and the 414, with features of both. By 1978 the Titan came out in a third version, the Freighter to haul freight alone.

Cessna has handily captured the old Beech 18 "mail plane" type market with enough different versions of the low-400 series to give anyone what he is looking for. The success of the series attests to its filling a need.

The aircraft are all straight-forward enough, but at full loads on hot days, the gap between V_{mc} and best single-engine climb speed is wide. Operators have had to look carefully at weight and performance graphs in flying them out of 3,000 ft or so to insure enough margin for safety.

Cessna's 401 Businessliner is an unpressurized six/eight-placer with office amenities and 2,500 pounds of hauling ability.

The Cessna 402 for 1977.

136

1972 Cessna Model 402B

Engines: Continental TSIO-520-E, 6-cylinders, fuel injected, rated 300 hp at 2,700 rpm

Gross weight:	6,300 lb	5,100 lb
Speed (best power mixture):		
Maximum at sea level	228 mph (198 kt)	236 mph (205 kt)
Maximum at 16,000 ft	261 mph (227 kt)	271 mph (236 kt)
Maximum recommended cruise, 75% power at 10,000 ft	218 mph (189 kt)	226 mph (197 kt)
Range:	660 mi	683 mi
Normal lean mixture:	3.05 h	3.05 h
maximum 75% power at 10,000 ft	216 mph (188 kt)	224 mph (195 kt)
600 lb usable fuel	1,186 mi	1,230 mi
No reserves	5.49 h	5.49 h
75% power at 10,000 ft	216 mph (188 kt)	224 mph (195 kt)
1,080 lb usable fuel	972 mi	1,014 mi
No reserves	4.12 h	4.12 h
75% power at 20,000 ft	236 mph (205 kt)	246 mph (214 kt)
840 lb usable fuel	1,454 mi	1,609 mi
No reserves	6.76 h	7.83 h
Maximum range at 25,000 ft	215 mph (187 kt)	205 mph (178 kt)
1,080 lb usable fuel		
No reserves	1,610 ft/min	2235 ft/min
Rate of climb at sea level:	225 ft/min	560 ft/min
Twin engine		
Single engine	26,180 ft	29,450 ft
Service ceiling:	11,320 ft	20,250 ft
Twin engine		
Single engine	1,695 ft	1,036 ft
Takeoff performance:	2,220 ft	1,361 ft
Ground run		
Total distance over 50-ft obstacle	6,200 lb	5,100 lb
Landing performance:	777 ft	509 ft
Landing weight	1,765 ft	1,497 ft
Landing roll	3,719 lb	3,719 lb
Total distance over 50-ft obstacle	590 lb	590 lb
Empty weight (approx.)	32.2 lb/sq ft	26.1 lb/sq ft
Baggage allowable	10.5 lb/hp	8.5 lb/hp
Wing loading		
Power loading		
Fuel capacity (total):		
Standard	102 gal (612 lb)	
Optional	143 gal (858 lb)	
Standard, optional, and wing locker fuel	184 gal (1,104 lb)	
Oil capacity (total):	6.5 gal	
Wing span:	39.86 ft	
Wing area:	195.7 sq ft	
Length:	35.83 ft	
Height:	11.68 ft	

137

Cessna Model 414 (1969–78)

Cessna has been the aggressive company in getting several different twins into the marketplace. Their 400 series is certainly proof of that, and the airplanes have found loyal owners. The 414 came out after all the other 400s, and in the same year the 411 was dropped as a pressurized medium twin second in line to the 421. In essence, the idea was a less costly 421 but something larger than the 340. Skeptics did not see that another "in between" airplane was needed, but the 414 has made it.

Buying a twin in the 414's category becomes a bit harder, since it is always "just under or just over" similar turbocharged, pressurized twins. Here the prospective owner-pilot must define his requirements very carefully to make sure he gets what he needs.

The 414s up through the 1977 models were five-people aircraft in IFR conditions for 800 mi at 225 mph. The 310-hp Continentals were good for sea-level power up to 20,000 ft, with either engine able to keep the cabin pressurized. They carried as many as six fuel tanks (only two were standard), and fuel management was bothersome—transfer pumps, monitor of fuel return, tank selection.

With the 1978 model year, Cessna turned the 414 into the Chancellor, a very different airplane even though labeled the 414A. What happened was a combination of the airframe developments of the 1976 Model 421 and the reliable Continental 310-hp engines that gave so much good service. Gross weight and useful load went up with higher cruising altitudes. Single-engine service ceiling jumped from 11,350 ft to 19,850 ft. The Chancellor with 310-hp engines cruises 6 mph faster and 25 percent more miles per gallon than the 1971 Model 421A, which had 375-hp engines. That new wing (bonded and wet) changed aspect ratio and area to give this boost in performance. The nose was also extended with more baggage space: the 414A is roomy as well in a cabin that stays at 6,000 ft when the airplane is at 20,000 ft. It handles very differently, too—very responsive and simple to fly and manage, with fingertip control.

If you are going to get into this "medium" class, look closely to see if these differences count for you.

The Cessna 404 Titan is aimed at the business, commuter, and air-taxi markets, with 375-hp engines and a 3,600-pound useful load.

The Cessna 414s have been five-people, IFR aircraft for 800 mi at 195 kt—until the 1978 model, called the Chancellor, upped this performance with a number of improvements.

1973 Cessna Model 414

Engines: Two 6-cylinder, fuel-injection engines, rated 310 hp at 2,700 rpm

Gross weight: 6,350 lb

Speed (best power mixture):
Maximum at sea level, 227 mph (198 kt)
Maximum at 20,000 ft, 272 mph (237 kt)
Maximum recommended cruise
75% power at 10,000 ft, 220 mph (191 kt)
75% power at 25,000 ft, 252 mph (219 kt)

Range (recommended lean mixture):
Maximum recommended cruise
75% power at 10,000 ft, 600 lb 644 mi (2.94 h)
No reserve
219 mph (190 kt)
75% power at 10,000 ft, 1,218 lb 1,308 mi (5.97 h)
No reserve
219 mph (190 kt)
75% power at 25,000 ft, 735 mi, 600 lb, 2.94 h
No reserve,
250 mph (217 kt)
75% power at 25,000 ft, 1,493 mi, 1,218 lb, 5.97 h
No reserve,
250 mph (217 kt)
Maximum range at 25,000 ft, 1,615 mi 1,218 lb, 7.19 h
No reserve, 225 mph (196 kt)

Rate of climb at sea level:
Twin engine, 1,580 ft/min
Single engine, 240 ft/min
Service ceiling:
Twin engine, 30,100 ft
Single engine, 11,350 ft
Takeoff performance:
Ground run, 1,695 ft
Total distance over 50-ft obstacle, 2,350 ft
Landing performance:
Landing roll, 805 ft
Total distance over 50-ft obstacle, 1,865 ft
Empty weight (approx.): 4,035 lb
Baggage allowable: 1,090 lb
Useful load: 2,315 lb
Wing loading: 32.4 lb/sq ft
Power loading: 10.2 lb/hp
Fuel capacity (total):
Standard, 102 gal
Optional (40-gal wing auxiliary tanks), 143 gal
Optional (63-gal wing auxiliary tanks), 166 gal
Optional (63-gal wing auxiliary tanks with locker transfer tanks), 207 gal
Oil capacity: 6.5 gal
Wing span: 39.86 ft
Wing area: 195.72 sq ft
Length: 33.75 ft
Height: 11.85 ft

Cessna Model 421 (1967–78)

The 421 has been another Cessna success story. Coming out of the 401 and 402 airframe, two 375-hp geared engines were hung on the wings and a real performer emerged into the turbocharged-pressurized market.

The first 421s had short noses, narrow gear, and 300 lb of fuel in the well-known Cessna canted tip tanks. By 1970 the B model was out and firmly established in the "big cabin, pressurized airplane at the lowest price" bracket. The B also came with a bigger nose, wider gear, a higher aspect ratio, and greater payload.

The geared engines became known as maintenance headaches, and 421s have been known to spend a considerable amount of time in the hangar with cracks in the crankcases, and upper cylinder problems. But, since the props turn at 2,275 rpm maximum in the older models, the result is less noise and fatigue.

139

The 421 comes in the plush executive Golden Eagle or the ten-place Executive Commuter version. Either way, the inside is comfortable: by 1973 pressurization was 5.0 psi, or an 8,000-ft cabin at 23,100 ft. It has always been a passenger pleaser.

In 1976 Cessna came out with, for all intents and purposes, a new machine in the 421C. The tip tanks were gone, and there were virtually no rivets in the new bonded wing (wet outboard of the nacelles). The vertical fin and rudder were extended, and higher performance props were added, as was a 5-sec hydraulic landing-gear system. The wet wing also eliminated the complex fuel management problems while upping capacity. A 2,949-lb useful load could be carried 1,251 nm at 75 percent power and 25,000 ft.

The 421 has always been known as a pilot's airplane that is not very difficult to fly. Handling is developed into a delight with the control pressures moderate and stalls very gentle. Passengers and pilots both like it. The major bugaboo comes to the systems, like the blowdown gear in the C (only once, then the whole system has to be reserviced), the too-warm cabin when pressurized at lower altitudes, and the engines. The upper cylinder problems have been primarily operator-induced, however. The cure is do not lean by the flight manual—go for 100° to 125° rich on the EGT and no rapid descents with power below 20–23 in. to the threshold.

Here is a top-of-the-line airplane for going in style. Look carefully before you invest.

The pressurized 421 Golden Eagle represents another Cessna success story, but its 375-hp geared engines have given some trouble.

1973 Cessna Model 421B

Engines: Two GTSIO-520-H, 6-cylinders, fuel-injected, rated 375 hp at 2,275 rpm

Useful load: 3,029 lb
Gross weight:
  Takeoff, 7,450 lb
  Landing, 7,200 lb
Speed (best power mixture):
  Maximum at sea level, 237 mph (206 kt)
  Maximum at 18,000 ft, 282 mph (245 kt)
  Maximum recommended cruise 75% power at 10,000 ft, 233 mph (202 kt)
  Maximum recommended cruise 75% power at 25,000 ft, 270 mph (235 kt)
Range (recommended lean mixture):
  Maximum recommended cruise, 75% power at 10,000 ft, 1,020 lb, 922 mi (3.99 h)
  No reserves, 231 mph (200 kt)
  75% power at 10,000 ft, 1,488 lb, 1,344 mi (5.82 h)
  No reserves, 231 mph (200 kt)
  75% power at 25,000 ft, 1,020 lb, 1,057 mi (3.99 h)
  No reserves, 265 mph (231 kt)
  75% power at 25,000 ft, 1,488 lb, 1,542 mi (5.82 h)
  No reserves, 265 mph (231 kt)
  Maximum range at 25,000 ft, 1,716 mi 1,488 lb, 7.27 h

No reserves, 236 mph (206 kt)
Rate of climb at sea level:
  Twin engine, 1,850 ft/min
  Single engine, 305 ft/min
Service ceiling:
  Twin engine, 31,100 ft
  Single engine, 13,000 ft
Takeoff performance:
  Ground run, 1,977 ft
  Total distance over 50-ft obstacle, 2,507 ft
Landing performance:
  Gross weight, 7,200 lb
  Landing roll, 720 ft
  Total distance over 50-ft obstacle, 2,178 ft
Empty weight (approx.): 4,421 lb
Baggage allowable: 1,500 lb
Wing loading: 35.20 lb/sq ft
Power loading: 9.93 lb/hp
Fuel capacity (total):
  Standard, 175 gal
  Optional auxiliary tanks, 202 gal
  Optional auxiliary tanks and wing locker tanks, 255 gal
Oil capacity (total): 6.5 gal
Wing span: 41.86 ft
Wing area: 211.65 sq ft
Length: 36.08 ft
Height: 11.58 ft

The Gulfstream-American Cougar was introduced in 1978 as a ''light, light'' twin—a four-placer with limited range but possessing outstanding handling characteristics.

Gulfstream-American Model GA-7 Cougar (1978–)

In 1978 Piper, Beech, and Gulfstream-American got their "light, light" twins on the market, with Cessna puffing not far behind. Ever since the Twin Comanche left the light, low-cost, efficient concept and grew to six places and a price 25 percent above high-performance singles, a gap has remained between the top singles and the bottom twins.

The Cougar (page 141) is a combination of honeycomb and metal-bonding techniques, with some standard riveting thrown in. It is a simple airplane to build, to operate, to fly. The most significant thing about it, though, is that V_{mc} is 2 kt under flaps-down stall speed of 63 kt. This makes single-engine work in it almost as easy as in the Skymaster. Then it gets up and goes 160 kt at 75 percent power and 8,500 ft with two 160-hp Lycomings. But remember, this is a light twin, four-seater. If one fills up the tanks there are around 550 lb left for people and baggage. But with some fuel out of the tanks, it can still take four people IFR for 300 nm.

The Cougar has very good stability and handling characteristics and a gear-extension speed of 145 kt. It is limited in IFR flying—no weather radar, airframe deice, or prop deice options came with it. Later the airplane might get them, along with two more seats, but that will definitely decrease useful load. There is no question that the manufacturers will be tempted to make it heavier and more powerful, and we might see history repeat itself as the price gets too high again.

Surprisingly, the GA-7 is larger than the Twin Comanche, with plenty of room, ample wing span, and good baggage room. The cabin, from firewall to the back of the rear seat, is 7.9 ft long, 3.75 ft wide, and 4.6 ft high. Passenger comfort has obviously been considered, but pilots will find their seat cushions too thin and uncomfortable after an hour or so.

The market is certainly open for the light, light twin with docile single-engine characteristics. Before you buy a high-performance single, see if you can fly one of the airplanes in this category to see if it suits your needs.

The last Twin Comanches built had counterrotating propellers.

1978 Gulfstream-American GA-7 Cougar

Engines: Two Lycoming O-320-D1D, 4-cylinders, 160 hp at 2,700 rpm (recommended time between overhauls, 2,000 h)

Maximum gross weight: 3,800 lb	Baggage limits:
Basic empty weight: 2,515 lb	Forward compartment, 75 lb
Useful load: 1,285 lb	Aft cabin compartment, 200 lb

142

Speeds:
Maximum at sea level, 194 mph (168 kt)
Maximum recommended cruise, 75% power at 8,500 ft, 184 mph (160 kt)
Maximum range cruise, 45% power at 8,500 ft, 132 mph (114 kt)
Stall (power off)
Flaps up, 82 mph (71 kt)
Flaps down, 72 mph (63 kt)
Minimum control speed, single engine, 70 mph (61 kt)
Takeoff performance (maximum gross weight, sea level, 59° F):
Total distance over 50-ft obstacle, 1,850 ft
Ground run, 1,000 ft
Rate of climb at sea level:
Twin engine, 1,200 ft/min
Single engine, 310 ft/min
Service ceiling:
Twin engine, 18,300 ft
Single engine, 4,900 ft
Landing performance (maximum gross weight, sea level, 59° F):
Total distance from 50-ft height, 1,330 ft
Ground roll, 710 ft
Range:
Range and endurance figures include allowances for start, taxi, takeoff, cruise climb to altitude, cruise, descent, plus fuel sufficient for 45 min of holding at 45% power.
Maximum recommended cruise speed, 118 gal, 75% power, 8,500 ft:
Endurance, 5.1 h
Range, 800 nm
Maximum recommended cruise speed, 80 gal, 75% power, 8,500 ft:
Endurance, 3.1 h
Range, 510 nm
Maximum range power, 118 gal, 45% power, 8,500 ft:
Endurance, 10.1 h
Range, 1,160 nm
Maximum range power, 80 gal, 45% power, 8,500 ft:
Endurance, 6.3 h
Range, 730 nm
Length: 29.84 ft
Height: 10.36 ft
Wing span: 36.86 ft
Wing area: 184 sq ft
Wing loading: 20.65 lb/sq ft
Power loading: 11.88 lb/hp
Fuel capacity, maximum: 118 gal
Oil capacity, each engine: 8 qt

Piper PA-30, 39 Twin Comanche (1963–72)

Just as Beech had to put two engines on their hottest single, the Bonanza, so Piper had to follow suit with the beautiful Twin Comanche. This airplane was the only twin that held the ''light, light'' portion of the market until it got too expensive and finally went out of production. It remains a favorite with pilots.

Up until 1970, the Twin Comanche was known as the PA-30; then another version came out with counterrotating propellers called the PA-39 C/R. This was the first time since the P-38 that such a feature had been incorporated into a production twin. Since that time, several twins have come out with it, eliminating the so-called critical engine.

Twin Comanches were known at times for training accidents, but these were caused, it was ascertained, by low-time instructors taking students not just down to V_{mc} on one engine but to the stall. Not much else could happen but a spin, and some went in. Since those days, the airplane has been cleared of any inherent fault by both NASA and the FAA.

The airplane is a fine performer, with two 160-hp Lycomings, nudging 200 mph at 75 percent power, burning but 20 gal/h. It is important to check that the alternators are on and working, since they can be knocked off with a foot in some versions. Since the aircraft has electric gear, nudging one off could mean no juice to get it down.

Wheelbarrowing is a tendency on both takeoff and landing, because of the stubby gear struts. The plane is tight and responsive on the controls and very quiet inside, which often surprises most first-timers. It usually falls to the left in stalls, and it is short-coupled with much mass out there on the wings; down toward the stall it does feel loose and slightly topheavy. At V_{mc} it requires a full bootful of rudder to keep straight, and even an engine failure at cruise produces significant yaw. There is no question that one must clean the airplane up before it will climb on one engine.

Tip tanks were options to boost a 90-gal capacity to 120 gal (standard on the Turbo Twin Comanche). They are great for range but add more mass out there on the wings to swing around.

This bird deserves a close look, especially the C/R, with its effortless climbs. Just remember it is small and will not have a sterling load-carrying capability.

1970 Piper PA-39 Twin Comanche C/R

Engines: Two Lycoming IO-320-B1A, 160 hp at 2,700 rpm

Gross weight: 3,600 lb
Empty weight: 2,270 lb
Useful load: 1,330 lb
Wing span: 36 ft
Wing area: 178 sq ft
Length: 25.2 ft
Height: 8.2 ft
Power loading: 11.25 lb/hp
Wing loading: 20.22 lb/sq ft
Baggage capacity: 250 lb
Fuel capacity: 90 gal
Stalling speed
  (flaps extended): 70 mph (62 kt)
Takeoff ground run: 940 ft
Takeoff distance
  over 50-ft obstacle: 1,530 ft

Landing ground roll: 700 ft
Landing distance
  over 50-ft obstacle: 1,870 ft
Accelerate-stop distance: 2,470 ft
Best rate-of-climb speed: 112 mph (97 kt)
Single-engine best rate-of-climb speed: 105 mph (92 kt)
Rate of climb at sea level: 1,460 ft/min
Rate of climb at 10,000 ft: 950 ft/min
Best angle-of-climb speed: 90 mph (78 kt)
Single-engine rate of climb: 260 ft/min
Ceiling: 20,000 ft
Single-engine ceiling: 7,100 ft
Top speed: 205 mph (178 kt)

	Cruise speed at opt. alt. (mph/kt)	Cruising range at opt. alt. (sm)	Fuel consumption (gal/h)
Normal cruise	198/172	830	19.6
Intermediate	196/170	1,030	15.4
Economy cruise	188/163	1,110	13.8
Long-range cruise	178/155	1,200	11.6

144

The Piper Apache is the cheapest and easiest twin to buy and fly, and probably the least useful. Pictured is the 1959 model.

The potato-shaped Apache, originally designed by Eddie Stinson, was one of those early general-aviation twin pioneers, along with the Cessna 310. But the Apache was endowed with less striking appearance and performance than the 310. She was ugly—but cheap to buy and fly, docile, and about the least useful plane unless one wanted to get a multi rating for the least money.

The first models had 150-hp engines that gave the airplane a bad case of being underpowered. Horsepower went up, the most common modifications being 170–180-hp Lycomings, vastly improving single-engine performance; but a hot day was still a bad omen. If the airplane was not cleaned up immediately when an engine was lost, then it just did not climb. As a matter of fact, the advice was often to look for a field straight ahead, since the plane, when fully loaded, would begin to sink rather quickly. Add to this the fact that the only hydraulic pump was on the left engine, and so if it went, then the gear had to be pumped down. Rudder trim? That crazy Piper crank on the ceiling that always got turned the wrong way initially.

True airspeeds in the 150–160-mph range are not super, but the engines are burning only 17 gal an hour. On both engines the Apache handles like a Cherokee, and it floats on landing if the round wing tips have not been replaced. Retrofitted Hoerner tips eliminated that. Most Apaches around have been used in multi training, and it has been said that if one earns his rating in an Apache, with those nightmarish single-engine characteristics, he can fly any twin.

In 1957, props and landing gear were changed. When 160-hp engines were put on, the gross weight went from 3,500 lb to 3,800 lb. If you find one of these, be sure to see if it has the half-inch valves that up TBO to 2,000 h. Check the rear fuselage bulkhead for corrosion and cracks; training meant full bashing of the rudders for single-engine work, and even the rudder hinges could be cracked. By 1960, gear speed was raised to 150 mph and flap speed to 125 mph. Apaches lack drains in the fuel cap recesses as well, so check for rust or even a hole that leaks water into the fuel tank. As it is, one can get water into the tanks by failing to check before fueling.

Without changing numbers, Piper finally turned the PA-23 into a different, much improved airplane, the Aztec. But the old Apache has her uses.

145

Apache 235.

Piper Apache 235
Engines: Two Lycoming O-540-B1A5,
　235 hp at 2,575 rpm
Gross weight: 4,800 lb
Empty weight (standard): 2,735 lb
Useful load (standard): 2,065 lb
Empty weight (AutoFlite): 2,850 lb
Useful Load (AutoFlite): 1,950 lb
Fuel capacity: 144 gal
Wing span: 37 ft
Wing area: 207 sq ft
Length: 27.6 ft
Height: 10.3 ft
Wing loading: 23.2 lb/sq ft
Power loading: 10.2 lb/hp
Baggage capacity (maximum): 200 lb
Baggage compartment space: 25 cu ft
Cargo space, rear seat removed: 80 cu ft
Gross weight: 4,800 lb
Top speed: 202 mph (175 kt)

Cruising speed at 75% power, 7,000 ft:
　191 mph (166 kt)
Stalling speed (power off, flaps down):
　62 mph (54 kt)
Takeoff run, 25° flaps: 830 ft
Landing roll (flaps down): 880 ft
Best rate-of-climb speed: 112 mph (97
　kt)
Rate of climb: 1,450 ft/min
Best single-engine rate-of-climb speed:
　110 mph (96 kt)
Single-engine rate of climb: 220 ft/min
Service ceiling: 17,200 ft
Single-engine absolute ceiling: 6,600 ft
Fuel consumption at 75% power: 28
　gal/h
Cruising range:
　75% power at 7,000 ft, 980 mi
　65% power at 11,000 ft, 1,100 mi
　55% power at 12,000 ft, 1,185 mi

**Piper
PA-23
Aztec
(1963–78)**

Putting the airplanes next to each other, it is plain to see that the Aztec is really the Apache much improved. Piper even kept the same model number, PA-23. Today the airfoil remains the same, but engines have become more powerful and a larger swept tail and a pointy nose have been added. But that airfoil gives the Aztec its progenitor's low takeoff and landing speeds and docility.

The rugged steel-tube structure surrounding the cabin remains as well, but it is heavy. In 1967 turbocharging came on the Aztec C, and the old dowager was up there among the best, doing 200 mph, carrying 140 gal usable fuel to go 1,200 mi. Not blistering, but certainly not bad.

With the Aztec F came a new stabilator of greater and higher aspect ratio, with external mass balances at the tips; and, finally, the round wing tips were replaced by Hoerner-type square ones that held another 20 gal of fuel.

146

The Piper Aztec is an improved version of the Apache.

Why the latter was not done before 1976 is a mystery, since mods of this type had been common for some time to improve landing characteristics of both the Apache and the Aztec. Another Piper trademark that has always irritated pilots for years held on—the elevator-trim hand crank in the ceiling. When operating it, one seems to inevitably crank it the wrong way at first no matter how much one uses it. Most Aztecs of later vintage came with electric trim, though, so the crank could be left alone. The new tail did bring a great reduction in stick force, much to pilots' delight.

Low flap and gear speeds (125 and 150 mph tops) have always bothered pilots when jets were breathing down their backsides on approaches, but one can get used to it. Slow flight in the Aztec is a delight, even below the V_{mc} of 80 mph, but single-engine flying shows its Apache ancestry: the left engine is not only "critical," but the hydraulic pump for the gear is still there, with a 50-stroke hand pump the only backup. The airplane will not climb out of ground effect with gear down and a windmilling prop; the decision to feather or to pump is a rough one that has no firm answer.

When looking into an Aztec, one must think about tolerant low-wing loading, an honest six seats, and ruggedness versus single-engine flying problems. Fly it a great deal single-engine before you buy.

1975 Piper PA-23 Aztec
Engines: Two Lycoming IO-540-C4B5 250 hp at 2,575 rpm
Top speed: 216 mph (188 kt)
Altitude cruise speeds:
Normal, at 4,000 ft, 210 mph (183 kt)
Economy cruise, at 6,400 ft, 204 mph (177 kt)
Stall speed, flaps extended: 68 mph (59 kt)
Takeoff: 820 ft
Takeoff over 50-ft obstacle: 1,250 ft
Landing: 850 ft
Landing over 50-ft obstacle: 1,250 ft
Accelerate-stop distance: 2,220 ft
Rate of climb: 1,490 ft/min
Best rate-of-climb speed: 120 mph (104 kt)
Single-engine rate of climb: 240 ft/min
Best single-engine rate-of-climb speed: 102 mph (88 kt)

Ceiling: 21,100 ft
Single-engine ceiling: 6,400 ft
Fuel consumption:
Normal, 34 gal/h
Economy cruise, 25 gal/h
Altitude cruise range:
Normal, at 4,000 ft, 830 mi
Long-range cruise, at 10,200 ft, 1,210 mi
Gross weight: 5,200 lb
Empty weight: 3,042 lb
Useful load: 2,158 lb
Wing span: 37.2 ft
Wing area: 206.6 sq ft
Length: 31.2 ft
Height: 10.3 ft
Power loading: 10.4 lb/hp
Wing loading: 25.05 lb/sq ft
Baggage capacity: 300 lb
Baggage compartment space: 46.7 cu ft
Fuel capacity (140 gal usable): 144 gal

The Piper Aztec F has a redesigned stabilator, Hoerner wingtips, and additional fuel capacity. Pictured is the 1978 turbo version.

147

Piper PA-31 Navajo (1967–78)

Ever since Piper decided to enter the cabin-class market with their Turbo Navajo (so called in 1967), the aircraft has been a real winner. Around 2,000 had been built a decade later, coming in three different versions.

The Navajo has always been an aerodynamically pleasing machine in looks and performance. Piper decided not to link any vital systems to just one engine (while persisting to do so with the Aztec and its gear) and the laminar flow wing was aerodynamically "twisted" for low stall speeds and good short-field capability. The CG range also turned out to be the widest in class.

The 1967 model had a 2,741-lb useful load with 230 mph at 16,000 ft and 75 percent power. The nonturbocharged version came with 300-hp Lycomings that gave 210 mph at 6,400 ft, maximum cruise with 2,597-lb useful load, but it was later dropped in favor of three versions with turbocharging.

Pressurization was soon added as an option, but it was eventually dropped, leaving the Cessna 421 to carry as much with no need for oxygen above 12,500 ft. The system proved to be a maintenance headache worse than the 421's system, but pressurized Navajos continue to serve. Carefully check the maintenance history if you plan to buy one.

In spite of the lack of pressurization, Piper has sold the Navajos to over 50 percent of the market for this class of airplane. It is comfortable and quiet, and pilots enjoy flying it. It is hard to misload, because of the generous CG range, and it can manage smaller fields without much problem. Single-engine flying is easier than in the Aztec.

By 1978 the five- or six-place Navajo had 310-hp engines, with a TBO of 1,800 h. The Navajo C/R (counterrotating propellers—very popular) had 325-hp engines, and the top-of-the-line Chieftain had 350-hp Lycomings, also with counterrotating props, with room for up to nine commuters or a nice office for executives. With a 221-kt top cruise speed, V_{mc} came down to 76 kt for this largest of Navajos, carrying 3,009 lb useful load.

With a long cabin and good handling, the Navajo bears looking at.

1971 Piper PA-31 Turbo Navajo B

Engines: Lycoming TIO-540-A, 310 hp at 2,575 rpm

Top speed, 15,000 ft: 261 mph (227 kt)

Altitude cruise speeds at 12,000 ft (hp per engine):
- 230 hp, 223 mph (194 kt)
- 200 hp, 208 mph (181 kt)
- 170 hp, 192 mph (167 kt)
- 140 hp, 170 mph (148 kt)

Stall speed: 73 mph (64 kt)

Normal takeoff ground run: 1,030 ft

Short-field takeoff ground run: 860 ft

Normal takeoff distance over 50 ft: 2,190 ft

Short-field takeoff distance over 50 ft: 1,700 ft

Normal landing ground roll: 1,915 ft

Short-field landing ground roll: 1,235 ft

Normal landing distance over 50 ft: 2,340 ft

Short-field landing distance over 50 ft: 1,810 ft

Accelerate-stop distance: 2,085 ft

Best rate-of-climb speed: 110 mph (96 kt)

Single-engine best rate-of-climb speed: 110 mph (96 kt)

Single-engine minimum control speed: 85 mph (74 kt)

Best rate of climb: 1,445 ft/min

Single-engine best rate of climb: 245 ft/min

Best angle-of-climb speed: 95 mph (83 kt)

Single-engine best angle-of-climb speed: 106 mph (92 kt)

Service ceiling: 26,300 ft

Single-engine service ceiling: 15,200 ft

Absolute ceiling: 27,300 ft

Single-engine absolute ceiling: 15,900 ft

Fuel consumption (total per hour, hp per engine):

230 hp at 2,400 rpm, 35.6 gal
200 hp at 2,300 rpm, 27.4 gal
170 hp at 2,200 rpm, 23.1 gal
140 hp at 2,200 rpm, 19.7 gal

	Cruising range with 190 gal	At 22,000–24,000 ft with 45-min reserve	At 12,000 ft with 45-min reserve
Horsepower per engine	230 hp at 2,400 rpm	1,110 mi	1,020 mi
	200 hp at 2,300 rpm	1,410 mi	1,290 mi
	170 hp at 2,200 rpm	1,540 mi	1,410 mi
	140 hp at 2,200 rpm	1,590 mi	1,490 mi

Maximum gross weight: 6,500 lb
Empty weight, standard: 3,849 lb
Useful load, standard: 2,651 lb
Wing span: 40.67 ft
Wing area: 229 sq ft
Length: 32.63 ft
Height: 13 ft
Power loading: 10.5 lb/hp
Wing loading: 28.4 lb/sq ft

Baggage capacity:
Fore, 150 lb
Aft, 200 lb
Total, 350 lb
Baggage space:
Fore, 14 cu ft
Aft, 22 cu ft
Total, 36 cu ft
Fuel capacity
Standard, 150 gal
With built-in auxiliaries, 192 gal

Piper PA-34 Seneca (1971–78)

Piper got back into the light-twin market in the early 1970s (the Twin Comanche was fast outgrowing this area) with the Seneca. The roomy PA-34 was basically a Cherokee Six with two engines hung on the wings. Unfortunately the models up through 1974 were not very good performers.

Made to overload (six-place seating), full gross weight dropped range to just over an hour (200 mi). Aileron and elevator pressures were horrendous, and the airplane had a built-in Dutch roll (gone by 1973) that drove pilots crazy, especially in IFR. Noise and vibration were also excessive, and pilots have generally considered the Twin Comanche a much better airplane than its Seneca successor up to 1975. Single-engine performance was almost dangerous at gross weight, removing to a great extent the safety margin of two engines. Engines also failed regularly. And it was slow (170 mph).

But there were many things going for the Seneca. It was very roomy and comfortable for passengers, and the rear doors for baggage and cabin access were beautifully designed. Several of the systems were well thought out—dual alternators, electrically driven hydraulics for gear operation with either engine, and counterrotating propellers. Robertson came out with a STOL kit that gave the Seneca a real boost in performance through full-span flaps and spoilers, lowering V_{mc} from 80 to 67 mph and giving sparkling short-field capability (something the airplane already had to some extent).

149

The real metamorphosis came, however, with the 1975 Seneca II. The four-cylinder Lycomings were replaced with six-cylinder turbocharged Continentals that held together and boosted speed to over 200 mph. The span of the ailerons was increased 12 in. and the rudder-aileron interconnect was removed, giving much improved control pressures and response. Counterrotating props remained, and the stiff nosewheel steering was improved. IFR range came up to an honest 500 mi. Handling was Cherokee docile.

The turbocharging brought its own problems, being supersensitive in manifold pressure—a slight change in airspeed or throttle setting can bring on a 10-minute battle of chasing the gauges (badly placed behind the yoke in 1975). Nonetheless, single-engine performance is decent and passenger comfort optimum. As long as you keep in mind that gross weights and range need to be traded back and forth, the Seneca can be considered a Cinderella turned Princess like the Skymaster.

1974 Piper PA-34 Seneca

Engines: Two Lycoming IO-360, 200 hp at 2,700 rpm

Top speed, sea level: 195 mph (170 kt)

Optimum cruise speeds:
    75% power, 186 mph (162 kt)
    55% power, 178 mph (155 kt)

Stall speed, flaps extended: 69 mph (60 kt)

Takeoff run: 890 ft

Takeoff distance over 50-ft obstacle: 1,235 ft

Landing roll: 705 ft

Landing distance over 50-ft obstacle: 1,335 ft

Accelerate-stop distance: 1,860 ft

Rate of climb: 1,360 ft/min

Single-engine rate of climb: 190 ft/min

Best rate-of-climb speed: 105 mph (91 kt)

Best single-engine rate-of-climb speed: 105 mph (91 kt)

Best angle-of-climb speed: 90 mph (78 kt)

Service ceiling: 19,400 ft

Single-engine service ceiling: 3,650 ft

Fuel consumption (total):
    75% power, 20.6 gal/h
    55% power, 16 gal/h

Optimum cruise range:
    75% power, 856 mi
    55% power, 1,050 mi

Gross weight: 4,200 lb

Standard-equipped empty weight: 2,599 lb

Useful load: 1,601 lb

Wing span: 38.9 ft

Wing area: 206.5 sq ft

Length: 28.5 ft

Height: 9.9 ft

Power loading: 10.5 lb/hp

Wing loading: 20.3 lb/sq ft

Baggage capacity:
    Fore, 100 lb
    Aft, 100 lb

Baggage compartment space:
    Fore, 15.3 cu ft
    Aft, 20 cu ft

Fuel capacity: 100 gal (95 gal usable)

Turbocharged and Pressurized Twins

150

Most of the aircraft discussed in this section on used twins have, at one time or another, come with turbocharging and several with pressurization. Aero Commander created their 600 series with these features, as did Piper Aerostar. Beech beefed up their line, especially the Baron (Duke came standard with both); and Cessna put turbos on the 310. Cessna grabbed a big chunk of the pressurized market with the low-cost T337G P-Skymaster,

The 1978 Piper Chieftain (foreground) and Navajo C/R with counterrotating propellers. Some older Navajos are pressurized and have proven to be maintenance headaches.

The Piper Seneca, built from 1971 through 1974, is basically the Cherokee Six with two engines and poor performance. New engines and other modifications make Senecas built since 1974 much better airplanes. Pictured is the 1978 Seneca II.

which comes close to being the ideal business airplane with speed, economy, comfort, and simplicity. Piper came out with a turbo Twin Comanche and Aztec and put turbos in the Seneca by 1975. The larger the twin, the more likely you will find turbocharging and pressurization in combination.

Before buying a twin, one should be aware of what these two features will and will not do. First of all, some aircraft come with mechanical or gear-driven superchargers, but they are more inefficient than the exhaust-driven turbos. On the 380-hp engine used in the Queen Air or Aero Commander 680, the gearing and supercharger gobble about 40 hp or more at normal power settings. Find out if you want to live with this. The turbo simply spins to pump its air to the engine, and it is basically one moving part versus a multitude of complex gears.

Generally speaking, a normally aspirated machine will reach a maximum cruise speed at around 6,500 ft (the altitude at which full throttle will not deliver 75 percent power), while a turbocharged machine will go much higher. But when one gets above 12,500 ft, there is the need for oxygen or pressurization—which costs more money to maintain. This has to be offset by one's need: if you want to quickly get above icing and weather, nothing climbs like a turbocharged machine (short of turboprops and jets). Most normally aspirated twins do not have much single-engine ceiling or a very high single-engine climb capability either. If you will be flying over high terrain or out of higher-density altitude fields (particularly out west), the turbos are fine insurance. Just remember that even though engine output can remain at sea-level power, wings and props will not; takeoff distances will be longer and climbs shallower.

Another factor is distance: if trips will be short enough not to allow a turbocharged aircraft to get to altitude, there is no sense in buying. Turbos also add heavy loads to engines, so find out if your prospective aircraft has an add-on kit or came from the factory so equipped. Factory-turbocharged engines had the power plant built for stress and higher oil temperatures; kit-built ones did not. This does not mean add-on kits are bad—one simply has 151 to treat them with more respect. Also get a good briefing on turbo technique to get the most out of it (overboosting or overspeeding is very bad for these engines). Keep watch on oil and cylinder-head temperatures and keep in mind that an EGT is mandatory for fuel economy and engine protection. Remember, these airplanes also gulp 40–55 gal/h, so they are not cheap to run. Performance charts must be used to get the best out of the engines. Most pilots baby their engines at 65 percent power to get long life.

One major asset to turbocharging is a gain in TAS at higher cruise for the same fuel consumption. A Cessna 421B at 5,000 ft goes 219 mph for 1,034 statute miles (sm). At 25,000 ft (same power setting), it goes 262 mph for 1,237 sm on the same amount of gas.

Add pressurization to turbocharging, and one has the capability to go high and fast in real comfort. Just make sure you need it, because increased complexity brings increased costs. Pressurization is accomplished by bleeding off air downstream of the compressor and routing it through a flow-limiting sonic venturi and then through an intercooler and an air conditioner before entering the cabin (not all twins have the air conditioner, and this can mean a very warm cabin until cooler altitudes are attained). There is also a rate controller to govern the amount of air going out of the pressure vessel or cabin. Most piston twins operate in the 4.2–5 psi range. The Pressurized Navajo had a creditable 5.5 psi, but it was dropped entirely from the Navajo line because of constant maintenance problems. The Cessna 421 is also known for causing headaches with pressurization-system maintenance, but apparently owners are willing to put up with it for the delivered performance.

If you are going to enter this class, expect to face more adverse weather; if you are not going to get out that often, then you might not need all this sophisticated stuff. The magic words are *approved for flight into known icing conditions*. Deice and anti-ice systems present more things to be maintained, but they provide good insurance for getting ice off or preventing it from forming on important parts of the airframe and propellers.

Handling at high altitudes will also be very different—thinner air, higher angles of attack—and generally unpleasant. An autopilot handles these altitudes far better than a pilot if a flight lasts over a couple of hours.

All in all, make sure you weigh the pros and cons of turbocharging and pressurization before you buy. Not only are turbochargers and pressurization expensive in themselves, but more systems are usually added to fly efficiently where the former will take you. Systems management is the name of the game when you move up into the rarefied air of modern piston twins. A pilot can no longer flip the master switch on: he is in the world of main DC load bus, DC transfer bus, and inverters.

Appendix I: Avionics

Without question, among the major frustrations in flying an airplane are unreliable radios and assorted black boxes. Just when you seem to need one of those infernal gadgets the most, it decides of its own free will to take a coffee break. Inheriting bad radios is a likely prospect in buying a used airplane, yet most buyers find themselves mystified by the avionics panel—what is good, what is obsolete, what works but will fail shortly, how much are they worth in relation to the seller's asking price?

There are basically two questions to ask yourself in relation to the avionics found in an airplane you want to buy: Will the avionics serve your purpose in use of the aircraft? What investment value do the radios have, if any?

The first question only you can answer. In this day of TCAs, ARTS II and III radar, required ELTs, transponders and encoding altimeters, most pilots are going to be forced into having a certain amount of radios to get into most airports around the major population centers. If one never goes cross-country a great deal, then one or no radios can be tolerated; but even basic VFR gets pilots into the need for basic Comm-Nav equipment, not to mention IFR flying. All this should bring you to the point of deciding if the radios in the airplane are worth keeping or if you should replace them.

How best to tackle this brings us to the second complex question. Most prospective pilots know very little about the values in avionics. The best way to start is to make a list of the avionics in the airplane you want to buy. Take it home, free of the emotion of the moment, where you can be objective about it.

The key here is knowing which of the avionics are on the verge of becoming obsolete and worthless. If they are close to this stage, deduct the prices involved from the purchase price, and then, if the airplane becomes yours, yank them out to sell. Used radios sell fairly well, since one man's junk is another's treasure. Then upgrade your panel.

Much of this has to do with maintainability. When tubes began to be replaced by solid-state technology in the late 1960s, the world of avionics was revolutionized. Reliability took a quantum jump, and the best buys in used radios are those early solid-state boxes. With the exception of the later tube types, such as the Narco Mk. 12, the tubes should be replaced by solid state if you want reliability. Tubes simply generate more heat and need realignment periodically. Solid state also draws less power, and one can really pack a whole panel on a smaller electrical system.

Take your list to a reliable repairman or avionics shop, but be careful. As in any other business, there are sharks around, and a good shop is worth finding for future maintenance as well. Find out how the shop goes about its work. Be skeptical yet friendly. After all, you are the one who may be flying an ILS down to minimums in solid rain and half-mile visibility when poor maintenance decides to make the box give up the ghost. I know of one specific case where the glide slope was *reversed* because of sloppy maintenance. Fortunately the pilot double-checked it in VFR weather before it commanded him to fly into the ground. In addition, some shops will not touch certain radios because of parts and service problems. Find this out before investing in a black box.

The tough part comes in pricing fairly. A good bet is to average the prices found in *Trade-A-Plane* and other such periodicals where used radios show up. This will give you at least a general idea of what to keep in mind. Naturally, the general condition, manufacturer's reputation, and, if possible, pilots who have used them all need to be considered. Great bargains are around, such as the Bendix RN221 Comm and 222 Nav, if service is available; but if it is not, then when they go out, you are stuck. That is the time to sell and upgrade.

After your pricing venture, knock 25 percent off and you will have a fair idea of what you have. Again, it cannot be stressed enough that one of the major expenses in owning an airplane is avionics repair. The best way to beat that is to get reliable radios in the first place.

Assuming you sell some of your avionics through the periodicals or the local bulletin board, buying replacements is admittedly a rough task. New units are great, but is your airplane low enough in value not to warrant expensive updating? A used radio must be inspected carefully. Pull off the cover to see if there is any damage or evident wear. Does it have the yellow tag from an authorized shop saying the radio is fit for use? If the yellow tag is not present, you may still have a fine radio, but it will have to go through a shop to meet legal standards. Even though a shop will charge a premium for its reworked avionics, it has to stand by it if it goes bad. But if you are careful, you can buy on the used market and with the help of a good A&P mechanic get the stuff installed.

Never throw your old radios away: sell them, since someone always needs things you may not.

As for good buys, Narco, King, and Edo-Aire are all reliable, although the last has a lower resale value (good when you are buying, bad when selling). Some of the best buys are Narco Comm 10 and 11 and Nav 10, 11, and 12 sets because of their dependability. The newer generation of avionics is simply not that much better than the first solid-state boxes. For $900 to $1,400 you can pick up a good Nav-Comm package.

ADFs from the older days are very plentiful, but stay

away from them unless you have access to someone who can work on those tube installations. The solid-state units are very good, so check what is selling if you need one.

Used transponders are generally a real pain. The prices for new ones have really become reasonable, and it would pay to buy one from a discount house rather than chance the headaches of cranky used units.

In DMEs, steer clear of the older models: they are hard to maintain, and the newer ones are not going to give you as much headache. Distance measuring operates on the pulse system, so make sure you need this kind of sophistication, and be careful in your selection of a used one.

Used radars have recently become the best buy in used avionics. Solid-state types of the late 1960s to mid-1970s are very reliable and simple to install. The RCA AVQ-45, 46, and 47 series and the King and Bendix non-digital types are very good bargains—as low as $800. Add about $300 to $500 for installation, and the price remains phenomenal when compared to a new one at more than $5,000. Needless to say, it is best to have a twin with a radome to get the package that low. Conversion or the new single-engine radar packages are not cheap at all.

Autopilots are all over the place, and there is little question that the most effective for the money is the wing-leveler hooked to a gyro. It can be of immense help in reducing pilot work load on long cross-countries or for IFR work. Most run less than $1,000 installed. Next come the single-axis autopilots that monitor two gyros.

These are very popular and good IFR copilots, but here the price climbs. The two-axes and three-axes boxes get on up in both price and complexity, and one must carefully consider need. The best reason for any autopilot is single-pilot IFR: if you do a lot of it, begin looking and flying. The different systems will show their good and bad points through a few approaches and some vectoring.

The new digital generation is proving to be reliable and safe. As their used prices get down a bit, they will be worth picking up. Seeing the actual number displayed brings hope in reducing the number of dial interpretation errors that have dogged pilots since clock faces have been flying.

The trend is bringing sophisticated avionics down to the single/light-twin area. The boxes are getting lighter, pull less current, and are cheaper in many respects than their granddaddies, which bodes well for all of us who want to equip our flying machines without getting a second mortgage on the house.

It all comes back to making sure the avionics fit your need and determining their value so that you can get a fair price on the used airplane they are in. Always make sure that an aircraft's electrical system will handle what you intend to put in later. A friend who knows avionics is also a super asset to help you be properly skeptical and avoid a bad buy.

Even though these are general ground rules, they will clear away some of the mystery that surrounds those black boxes enough to give you a start. Good hunting!

Appendix II: Bluebook of Used Aircraft Prices

Pricing used airplanes is a real circus. One can equip an airplane with the most basic instruments and avionics or chock it full of the latest gadgets, which can double its value. Engine times since major overhaul, different engines, modifications, total airframe time, paint, interior, and so many other factors figure into the price of a used airplane that one simply has to shop for what one wants until something comes along that looks right for the money.

This does not help the buyer or the seller much, and aircraft prices are continually in a state of flux, to add to the confusion. In this section I must stress the word *average,* since there are so many variables. *Average* means basically equipped for that particular aircraft, in good shape, mechanically sound, and with mid-time engines.

Let it be stressed that this list of prices is not to point out the fair market value of the aircraft as it stands. The idea is to show you how much you should consider in spending for a certain type, knowing you will have to inflate or deflate that price according to what you want.

Another factor about the list should be obvious: the time required to get it in print will make it somewhat outdated. In short spans of time, aircraft prices change—some planes appreciate in value, others depreciate.

Regardless of the many factors involved, this list will give you a basic idea of what to expect when you look for "your" airplane.

Used Two-Place Airplanes

Aeronca Champion, Models 7AC, 7BCM, 7CCM, 7DC
  1945–50: $3,000 to $5,500
Aeronca Super Chief, Model 11AC
  1946–50: $3,000 to $5,500
Beechcraft Sport, Model 19
  1966–78: $8,000 to $35,000
Cessna 120 and 140
  1946–51: $4,000 to $6,000

Cessna 150 and Aerobat
  1959–77: $4,000 to $12,000
                  + $500 for Aerobat
Cessna 152
  1978: $14,000 to $19,000
Champion Traveler 7EC, Tri-Traveler, and Challenger 7GCB
  1955–62: $3,300 to $4,500 (7EC)
  1959–64: $4,000 to $5,500 (7GCB)
Champion Citabria, Models 7ELA, 7ECA, 7GCAA, 7KCAB, and 7GCBC

  1964–78: $5,200 to $15,500 (7ECA)
  1967–78: $7,000 to $21,000 (7GCB)
  1968–78: $8,500 to $19,000 (7KCAB)
  1968–78: $7,000 to $18,000 (7GCAA)
Champion Decathlon, Model 8KCAB
  1971–78: $12,000 to $22,000
Champion Scout, Model 8GCBC
  1975–78: $15,000 to $21,000
Ercoupe/Aircoupe
  1946–67: $4,200 to $5,000
                  $8,000 to $9,000 for Mooney

Great Lakes 2T-1A-1 and 2T-1A-2
  1973–78: $20,000 to $39,000

Gulfstream-American Yankee/Trainer
AA1, TR2, Lynx, and T-Cat
  1969–78: $6,500 to $18,000
  1972–78: $7,500 to $17,500 (TR2)

Luscombe Silvaire, 8A, 8E, and 8F
  1937–60: $4,000 to $5,500

Mooney Mite, Model 18
  1949–55: $3,700 to $6,000

Piper Cub, J-3, Super Cub, and PA-18
  1938–78: $5,500 to $22,000
  1960: $11,000

Piper Cruiser, J-5, Super Cruiser, J-5C,
and PA-12
  1941–48: $6,500 to $7,500

Piper Vagabond, PA-15 and PA-17
  1948: $6,500

Piper Colt, PA-22-108
  1961–63: $4,500 to $4,750

Piper Cherokee 140B, Flite Liner,
Cruiser, and PA-28
  1962–78: $5,800 to $22,000
  1970: $10,000

Pitts Special S-1S and S-2A
  1971–78: $15,000 to $28,000 (S-1S)
  1972–78: $25,000 to $34,000 (S-2A)

Taylorcraft BC-12D and F-19
  1946–47: $3,600 (BC-12D)
  1974–78: $10,000 to $13,000 (F-19)

Temco (Globe) Swift GC-1B
  1946–50: $10,000

Varga Kachina (Morrisey/Shinn 2150)
  1950–63: $6,000
  1974–78: $12,000 to $19,250

Used Four/Six-Place Airplanes, Fixed Landing Gear

Aero Commander 100, Darter and Lark
  1965–71: $6,000 to $12,000

Beechcraft Musketeer, Model 23,
Custom, Super, Sundowner
  1963–78: $7,500 to $32,000

Cessna 170, 170A, 170B
  1948–56: $7,000 to $10,000

Cessna 172 and Skyhawk
  1956–78: $7,000 to $30,000
  1969: $13,000

Cessna 175/Powermatic (Skylark)
  1958–63: $8,000 to $9,000

Cessna 180 and 185 Skywagon
  1953–78: $14,000 to $37,000 (180)
  1961–78: $16,000 to $42,000 (185)

Cessna 182 and Skylane
  1956–78: $11,000 to $38,000
  1967: $19,000

Cessna 177 Cardinal
  1968–78: $12,000 to $40,000

Cessna 205, 206, 207, Stationair
  1963–78: $18,000 to $65,000

Gulfstream-American Traveler, Cheetah,
Tiger
  1972–78: $13,500 to $30,000

Maule M-4 and M-5 Rocket
  1962–78: $7,000 to $26,000
  1970: $15,000

Piper Pacer PA-20 and Tri-Pacer PA-22
  1950–54: $3,700 to $5,000 (PA-20)
  1951–60: $4,750 to $6,625 (PA-22)

Piper Cherokee PA-28, Models 140 to
180, Archer, and Warrior
  1964–78: $7,200 to $22,000 (140)
  1963–75: $11,000 to $24,000 (180)
  1974–78: $16,000 to $25,000 (Warrior)
  1978 Archer: $30,000

Piper Cherokee 235 and Pathfinder
  1964–78: $14,000 to $42,000

Piper Cherokee Six 260 and 300, PA-32
  1965–78: $19,000 to $52,000 (300 +
            $2,000)

Stinson Voyager 108-1 and Station
Wagon 108-2
  1946–49: $6,000 to $7,000

Used Single-Engine, Retractable-Gear Airplanes

Aero Commander (Meyers) 200
  1959–67: $19,000 to $30,000

Beechcraft Bonanza Model 35
  1947–56: $13,000 to $18,000
  1957–63: $22,500 to $33,000
  1964–69: $38,000 to $47,500
  1970–78: $49,000 to $85,000

Beechcraft Debonair/Bonanza Model 33
  1960–67: $23,000 to $40,000
  1968–78: $35,000 to $80,000

Beechcraft Bonanza Model 36
  1968–78: $47,000 to $90,000

Beechcraft Musketeer Super R and
Sierra 200
  1970–78: $19,000 to $44,000

Bellanca Model 260 and Viking, Super
Viking 300
  1964–78: $16,000 to $55,000 (300 +
            $2,000)

Cessna 210 and Centurion
  1960–78: $18,000 to $67,000

Cessna 177 Cardinal RG
  1971–78: $21,000 to $43,000

Cessna Skylane RG
  1978: $55,000

Lake Buccaneer LA-4-200
  1957–78: $9,000 to $42,000

Mooney Mk. 20, 21, Ranger, and
Statesman
  1955–78: $6,000 to $38,000
  1968: $20,000

Mooney Super 21, Chaparral, and
Executive, 201
  1964–78: $18,000 to $42,000
           201: + $8,000

Navion and Navion Rangemaster
  1946–51: $10,000 to $12,000
  1960–76: $13,000 to $45,000

Piper Comanche 180, 250, 260, and
PA-24
  1958–72: $17,000 to $40,000 (180)
  1965–72: $27,000 to $40,000 (260)
  1964: $34,000 (400)

Piper Cherokee Arrow 180, 200, PA-28R,
Arrow II & III
  1967–78: $18,000 to $45,000

Piper Lance and Lance II
  1976–78: $55,000 to $64,000

Republic Seabee RC-3
  1948: $15,000

Rockwell Commander 112 and 114
  1972–78: $24,000 to $45,000 (112)
  1976–78: $45,000 to $57,000 (114)

Used Single-Engine Turbocharged Airplanes

Beechcraft Turbo Bonanza
  1966–70: $43,000 to $52,000

Bellanca Turbo Viking 300
  1969–78: $25,000 to $65,000

Cessna Turbo Super Skylane
  1966–71: $20,000 to $28,000

Cessna Turbo Stationair
  1972–78: $36,000 to $55,000

Cessna Turbo Skywagon
  1966–72: $24,000 to $35,000

Cessna Turbo Centurion
  1966–78: $30,000 to $76,000

Cessna Pressurized Centurion
  1978: $120,000

Lake Turbo Buccaneer
  1972–78: $40,000 to $65,000

Piper Turbo Comanche
  1966–71: $35,000 to $43,000

Piper Turbo Arrow III
  1977–78: $48,000 to $55,000

Rockwell 112TC-A
  1974–78: $38,000 to $50,000

Used Reciprocating Twin-Engine Airplanes

Aero Commander (Rockwell) 500, 600,
and 700 series
  1952–54: $18,000 to $20,000 (520)
  1954–64: $23,000 to $48,000 (560)
  1958–78: $30,000 to $220,000 (500)
  1958–60: $42,000 (720)

Aerostar 600 series
  1969–78: $80,000 to $150,000

Beechcraft Model 18
  1937–69: $18,000 to $53,000

Beechcraft Model 50 Twin Bonanza
  1952–62: $20,000 to $42,000

Beechcraft Model 95 Travel Air
  1958–68: $28,000 to $48,000

Beechcraft Model 55 and 58 Baron
  1961–78: $33,000 to $125,000 (55)
  1970–78: $80,000 to $165,000 (58)

Beechcraft Model 65, 70, 80, and 88
Queen Air
  1959–78: $63,000 to $300,000

Beechcraft Model 60 Duke
  1968–78: $105,000 to $290,000

Beechcraft Model 76 Duchess
  1978: $100,000

Cessna 310 and 320
  1954–78: $18,000 to $125,000 (310)
  1962–67: $31,000 to $55,000 (320)

Cessna 336 and 337 Skymaster
  1964: $16,500 (336)
  1965–78: $23,000 to $90,000 (337)

155

Cessna 340
  1972–78: $103,000 to $195,000
Cessna 401, 402, 404, and 411
  1965–78: $68,000 to $275,000
Cessna 414
  1969–78: $108,000 to $250,000
Cessna 421
  1967–78: $90,000 to $310,000
Gulfstream-American GA-7 Cougar
  1978: $75,000
Piper Twin Comanche, PA-30, 39
  1963–72: $28,000 to $47,000
Piper Apache, PA-23
  1954–65: $14,000 to $26,000
Piper Aztec, PA-23
  1960–78: $21,000 to $125,000
Piper Navajo, PA-31
  1967–78: $83,000 to $205,000
    (1975 on: C/R + $10,000)
  1973–78: $145,000 to $235,000
    (Chieftain)
Piper Seneca, PA-34
  1972–74: $37,500 to $43,000
  1975–78: $70,000 to $100,000 (Seneca
  II with turbo)

Piper PA-44 Seminole
  1978: $85,000

Used Twin-Engine Turbocharged and Pressurized Twin-Engine Airplanes

Note: Several of the twins listed before this section came with turbocharging and pressurization as standard features and were not included in this last list.

Aero Commander (Rockwell) 600 series
  1955–63: $28,000 to $47,000
  1962–69: $60,000 to $80,000 (680FP)
  1964–67: $81,000 to $90,000 (680FLP)
  1966–69: $120,000 to $153,000
  1972–74: $162,000 to $180,000
    (685 Pressurized)
Aerostar 601P and Turbo 601
  1974–78: $165,000 to $225,000
    (Pressurized)
  1969–78: $96,000 to $170,000 (Turbo)
Beechcraft Turbo Baron and Pressurized Baron

  1967–71: $59,000 to $68,000 (Turbo
    Baron)
  1976–78: $165,000 to $195,000
  1976–78: $188,000 to $240,000
    (P-Baron)
Beechcraft Model 88 Queen Air
  1966–67: $100,000 to $110,000
Cessna Turbo 310
  1969–78: $57,000 to $155,000
Cessna T337G Pressurized Skymaster
and Turbo Skymaster
  1973–78: $60,000 to $125,000
    (Pressurized)
  1967–78: $31,000 to $115,000 (Turbo)
Piper Turbo Twin Comanche
  1966–72: $39,000 to $51,000
Piper Turbo Aztec
  1966–78: $42,000 to $140,000
Piper Turbo and Pressurized Navajo
  1967: $83,000 (Turbo)
  1970–77: $118,000 to $293,000
    (P-Navajo)

Index

Figures in *italics* indicate illustrations.